Secrets of the Pelvis for Martial Arts:
A Practical Guide for Improving Your Wujifa, Taiji, Xingyi, Bagua and Everyday Life

By Michael Buhr

Copyright © 2013 by Michael Buhr

All rights reserved. No portion of this book, except for a brief review, may be reproduced, stored in a retrieval system or transmitted in any form, or by any means – electronic, mechanical, photocopying, recording, or otherwise - without written permission from the author.

Cover Design by Michael Buhr

Printed by CreateSpace, Charleston, SC

First Paperback Edition

ISBN-13: 978-1492149996
ISBN-10: 1492149993

Disclaimer

The information presented in this book is based on the personal experience and research of the author and is meant for educational purposes only. It is not a substitute for professional medical advice. The author and publisher of this material are not responsible in any manner whatsoever for any injury which may occur through reading and implementing ideas presented herein. Consult your personal healthcare provider before attempting any of the ideas presented in this book.

As an internal martial arts practitioner, the author has made a sincere effort to compile accurate and reliable information, but does not guarantee that the information presented is complete or appropriate for your specific situation.

Acknowledgements

Thank you to all my teachers, school brothers and sisters, students and martial art friends from whom I've learned over these last three decades.

A special thank you to my long-time mentor, friend, and founder of Wujifa, Richard J. Taracks whose functional approach to developing internal strength has helped me achieve the level of skill and understanding I have today. Without his encouragement this book would never have been written.

A Note from the Author

This title was originally published as an e-book in March 2013. The work you are holding is the paper edition of the same title.

Man has become absorbed with the upper portions of the body in intellectual pursuits and in the development of skills of hand and speech. This, in addition to false notions regarding appearances or health, has transferred his sense of power from the base to the top of his structure. In thus using the upper part of the body for power reactions he has reversed the animal usage and has to a great extent lost both the fine sensory capacity of the animal and its control of power centered in the lower spinal and pelvic muscles.
Mabel Elsworth Todd (1880-1956) in, The Thinking Body (pg. 160) first published in 1937. http://www.ideokinesis.com/pioneers/todd/todd.htm

Table of Contents

About the Author	ix
Preface	xi
1. Introduction	1
2. Paradigms and Worldviews	5
3. Wujifa: The Way of Connection	9
4. Visualization, Feeling and Tucking Under	11
5. Relaxing the Waist and Abdominal Breathing	13
6. Introducing the Crotch, Waist, and Hips	15
7. Qigong or Not Qigong	19
8. Internal Strength - Whole-body Connectedness	21
9. Comfort Level 1: Basic Data about Your Pelvis	27
10. Identifying Chronic Tension	35
11. Comfort Level 2: Locating Your Pelvis Externally	43
13. Rounding the Crotch	51
14. Comfort Level 3: Working with Your Pelvis Internally	57
15. Brief Introduction to Mind-Body, Psycho-Somatics	67
16. Comfort Level 4: Experiencing Your Pelvic-Emotional Connection	75
17. Conclusion	83
Appendix A: References to Crotch, Waist, Hips in Martial Arts	87
Excerpts from Books and Articles in English	87
Excerpts and Translations from Chinese Articles	108
Appendix B: Qigong - Excerpts from Books and Articles in English	129
Appendix C: American-Chinese Cross-Cultural Analysis of Round	137
Appendix D: Historical Use of Medical Rectal Dilators	147
Appendix E: Chinese Martial Arts Magazines in China	155
References	157

About the Author

Thread one. I was the little kid on the merry-go-round who got more enjoyment out of watching how it worked than I got out of the simple experience of the ride. "How does it work?" became a central theme in my life. I grew up with mechanical building toys and plastic models - plans, parts, assembly - how stuff went together. Later I graduated into big-boy toys; car repair, electronics, home mechanics. How does it work? I approach life pretty mechanistically.

Thread two. Standing in line my first day of kindergarten, the kid in front of me asked me what grade I was in. I said, "Kindergarten". He said, "You're too tall for kindergarten. You flunked." I ran home crying. I remained a head taller than my peers as well as gangly and uncoordinated through high school. I slouched to try to conceal my height. I just wanted to fit in and not feel like a mis-fit. Later in high school I had knee surgery from a sledding accident and multiple sprained ankles from playing basketball.

Thread three. I was the preschooler who got a Disney comic book written in Kanji; the seed of my fascination with Asia. I loved the 1970's TV show "Kung-fu" with David Carradine; the root of my fascination with Chinese martial arts. Later, when I got to college...

- One semester and a yellow belt in Judo.
- One year of Sofia Delza's dance-like Wu style Tai-chi Chuan with Professor Neville.
- Four years of William C.C. Chen's Yang style Tai-chi Chuan with Bob Klein.
- A bachelor's degree in Religious Studies with an interest in Asian philosophy.
- A year in China teaching English and practicing Tui-shou with a Chen stylist student, Yang Rui-wei.
- A few months with Gary Torres learning a Yang style Tai-chi two-person fighting form.
- Worked with Erle Montague and trained from almost 30 of his videos for two years.

- Workshops in Gao style Baguaquan with Victor Chou.
- Workshops in Xingyiquan and spear with Yan Gaofei.
- Workshops in Chen Silk Reeling, Laojia, and Tui-shou with Chen Xiao-wang.
- And now over ten years with Richard Taracks who, as I like to say, "cracked the code" in learning, demonstrating and teaching how to develop internal strength using simple, functional methods explained in plain English. His system is called Wujifa.

These are the experiences that I bring to the table. Ironically, I would have quit long ago if weren't for Mr. Taracks responding to my assertion that now I know (conceptually) how internal strength works. He said, "If you can't demonstrate it, then you really don't really know how it works." Rationally, I couldn't argue. And so I continued practicing and to date I've learned far more about "how it works" than when I thought I knew "how it works".

Maybe more important than knowing *how* it works is having learned through experience what stands in the way of "getting it". From childhood, I've identified with being mechanical; understanding the mechanics of things in this world. But to make progress in the internal martial arts requires ever deepening levels of feeling; something I had disassociated from long ago, something that to this day is still really uncomfortable and sometimes scary for me. Even though in Wujifa class my instructor has repeatedly guided me to feeling internal connectedness, I resist practicing and living my daily life with that level of feeling and openness. Consequently I'm taking much longer to "get it" than it should take, but that's me.

As of this writing, I live near Ann Arbor, Michigan, USA. I've been blogging my training experience and insights since 2009 at: internalgongfu.blogspot.com.

You can reach me at: internalgongfu@gmail.com. I would love to hear your comments about this book and ideas for a future edition.

Preface

Many sports are played at many levels. Children and teenagers can participate in a variety of sports. Adults can play sports their entire lives as hobbyists or enthusiasts. Some sports can also be played by Olympic or professionally trained athletes. The internal martial arts are exactly the same. They can be played at many levels from beginners to masters. However, there is one key difference between sports and internal martial arts. The higher the level the sport, the more refined the muscular coordination. The highest levels of the internal martial arts develop an entirely different kinesthetic skillset.

While the whole "internal style" and "external style" nomenclature has been popularized as a convenient way to describe the primary training directives of Chinese martial art styles, my experience has taught me that it is more functional to consider any of these styles in terms of the demonstrated kinesthetic skillsets of the individual performer. By kinesthetic skillsets I mean an underlying physical quality and not how pretty their forms look or how effective their techniques are. For example, an "internal" style can be performed externally by novice and master alike while an "external" stylist may move more internally than a less experienced "internal" stylist. Just because you are practicing an "internal style" does not mean that you are doing it internally!

I've heard it said in the martial arts that use belt systems that a black belt is not the highest level; it is the level where you now have the tools to begin learning. This is equally true in the "internal" styles, but in a different way. The tools needed to begin learning are not based on gross motor coordination skills and proficiency in demonstrating forms, techniques, and applications.

In my experience, the path from external to internal went through many levels beginning with learning gross muscular coordination of the forms, to refining this muscle coordination, to practicing zhan zhuang stance and learning about relax with structure, to getting lots of Rolfing massage for releasing fascial adhesions, to doing some psycho-somatic work to reduce my mind-body disassociation; increase my mind-body integration. Although none of this mind-body integration work directly resulted in the development of that unique kinesthetic quality known as internal strength, I now understand and consider it the preparatory work to get my body and mind to a place, to a level of sensitivity, to a level of feeling where I could begin learning.

In Taijiquan, one of the higher level kinesthetic skillsets is called "peng". In Wujifa, this quality is called "connection"; whole-body connection. To achieve this kinesthetic quality requires working beyond a child's or hobbyist's interest. It requires a meticulous Ph.D. level of attention to the minutest of details regarding emotional-muscular holding and letting go.

In my opinion, it is unfortunate that the internal martial arts were popularized in the U.S. alongside New Age concepts and Asian philosophical and medical paradigms: Tao, Yin-Yang, Qi, meridians, acu-points, spirituality, mysticism, healing, etc… Why do I say this? Because it is too easy to get absorbed into the mystical-philosophical aspect and remain disassociated from the body all the while *believing* that progress is being made. I have seen practitioners and teachers whose words were based on conceptual understanding and not connected to their kinesthetics. Their words said one thing and their bodies said another. These folks are everywhere. I have also seen teachers whose words and bodies were congruent; their words tried to convey what their bodies were demonstrating. These folks are few and far between.

The internal martial arts have been in the United States for about forty years and are now more widely practiced than ever and yet how many practitioners and teachers have we produced in these four decades that can functionally demonstrate internal strength? Very, very few. Why is this?

Based on my personal experience and observations, I contend that most practitioners and teachers don't make functional progress because they are stuck in their social-cultural taboos regarding the pelvis and are distracted by the New Age appropriation of and the mystical element of Asian philosophy, a.k.a., Taoism. Getting past those components and approaching internal training from a practical, functional perspective was a difficult process for me but one which is yielding the results I was looking for.

I think this book will provide internal martial artists with the information that is not talked about in the typical, public internal martial arts class. Because I obviously have not been an "indoor student" to every high-level teacher, I can't possibly know what methods are shared in strict confidence. If teachers and students are willing to share their teachings with me, I think this might make for an even more interesting second edition.

I hope that my nearly thirty years of experience, recent research for this book, and the excerpts that I quote will inspire you to further your own investigation into how your internal martial art skill level can be improved through employing simple, practical methods that, as I discovered, are widely known in the medical, massage, and physical therapy fields but are not openly discussed nor published in the internal martial arts community.

1

Introduction

My Wujifa instructor likes to tell this story: There are many paths up the mountain. When you get to the top, you will find the immortals laughing and singing and arguing about which path was the best.

The perspective you will read here is one of many paths. It is not the path I started on. It may not be the path you are currently taking. It is a path I switched to because I wasn't getting the results I wanted. You may discover this too.

The orientation of this book is primarily based on my training in Wujifa. In this book I relate my personal experience as well as my research on the pelvis. Therefore, my views may differ from recommended Wujifa practices.

This book is not a guide to stretching or building muscle or about how to develop magic Qi powers. Nor is it about how to improve your techniques or applications. While there are many books, videos and teachers that discuss these topics, from what I have seen, few if any get into details about working with the pelvis. I find it ironic that so many teachers and authors talk about the importance of "moving from the center" and "using the hip" but no one talks candidly and openly about those more personal aspects of "the center" that are supposed to drive our movement. Why is that? Shame? Fear? Social stigma?

Before we go further, be clear about your purpose; why you are training. Many of the externally oriented martial art stylists who need workable applications and techniques right now might find the information in this book to be unnecessary, useless or even frivolous. And I would agree with them. However, for the dedicated internal martial artist who is trying to develop a particular *quality* of internal movement, obsessing about meticulous details is a high priority.

While researching what others have written both in English and in Chinese about the pelvic area, namely, the waist, hips, crotch, and pelvic floor, I found that most English articles that address the pelvis address symptomatic clinical issues generally related to childbirth, incontinence or sexual dysfunction. This is likely due to historical trends. More recently books and articles are becoming available that address the biomechanics of the pelvic floor. And still, among American internal martial artists, there is practically nothing written. I was pleasantly surprised to find that Chinese internal martial artists write openly about the crotch and how it should function to develop internal strength. But even there, I found nothing in the way of methods or paths to achieving the desired functionality!

And so while it is widely recognized that the entire pelvic area (waist, hips, and crotch) is a key driver of movement in the internal martial arts, there are few if any authors who provide practical, functional methods to achieve the desired results. And so it's no surprise that a practical, down-to-earth understanding of how connecting with your pelvis can improve the power of your internal martial art skillset remains a bit of a mystery if not an outright "secret".

My goal in this book is to tastefully convey these so-called "secrets". Some of this is based on my experience working with this part of my body for many years and some is based on research into other's exercises that seem to me to serve this purpose. What you are about to read has been many years in the making.

Because of the "private" nature of the part of the body being discussed, you may find some of this information objectionable. If you do, then your reaction is likely very similar to my initial reaction when I first heard about this in Wujifa class. My intention is to inform, not to offend. If you find yourself feeling offended, you may have discovered your "Achilles Heel" in your practice. You may not be ready to act on this information now and that's O.K. Just keep in mind that not addressing your pelvis in a personal way may prevent you from making the progress you want to make.

This may be a book you read, set aside for a number of years, and then come back to when you are ready; after you let go of the mental resistance blocking this learning. It took me a more than a year to simply

Introduction

get comfortable with the mere idea that it is O.K. to work on relaxing this part of my own body! External family, social and cultural taboos created a huge internal psychological blockage! Getting over this conceptual and emotional hurdle was the first step for me. After I got comfortable with the mere idea of working "down there", it took me even longer before I acted on the idea and began taking active steps to work on relaxing my pelvic floor. And so, this may be a long process for you too. The very fact that you are reading this book suggests you have a level of openness to the idea of working with your pelvis.

Those whose studies or careers are in the medical, therapeutic, sports, or movement science fields may already have a level of comfort with the body overall and the pelvis in particular. However, there are many in the internal martial arts (like me) that have only a rudimentary knowledge of basic physiology and anatomy. In both cases, there will be those who have not done deeper work on themselves and may have maintained a level of mind-body disassociation. At this writing, I know that I am maintaining a level of disassociation too. But after years of trying to more fully integrate, I have a pretty good idea of where and how I am stuck. I offer a mix of my own experience up to where I am as of this writing and what I think might be a very practical and functional path inward.

The seven chapters following this introduction should give you an overview to the orientation of this book. Following this orientation, I've organized the core of this book according to what I believe are emotional comfort levels. To the extent that most people, like myself, tend to have some degree of disassociation from their bodies, taking incremental steps to introduce you to your pelvis seems like a good way to go. The information that is the most emotionally safe to me is presented first, namely, impersonal, mechanistic textbook data. This is Comfort Level 1. Each successive Comfort Level chapter delves deeper into integrating body-mind, you-pelvis. Comfort Level 5 is the most challenging or maybe the most uncomfortable. (This is generally where I'm stuck now.) The chapters interspersing the Comfort Level chapters are transitional chapters, related to both the previous and following Comfort Level chapter. The appendices substantially support and supplement the central tenet of this book. In fact, the appendices were originally included as chapters but I moved this information to appendices to condense the key points of the book and make this a quicker read.

I have discovered over the years that I work to whatever level I feel most comfortable or to whatever level suits my purpose at that time. You may discover this too. Sometimes where I stop, quit, or withdraw is where I find myself saying, "This is stupid! This has nothing to do with internal martial arts!" Upon reflection, I often learn that I encountered a fear about re-connecting with myself at that level. You may discover this too. Is it possible to work through something rather quickly? Sure. Is it possible to be stuck in the same place for years? Sure. From what I've seen, progress in the internal martial arts, or the lack thereof, depends both on how willing you are to relax and let go vs. how tenaciously you resist and hold onto existing emotional-muscular patterns.

2

Paradigms and Worldviews

In my years of learning different internal gong-fu forms and other practices, I recognize now in hindsight that I primarily saw and learned the superficial, mechanical differences of the physical technologies without deeply understanding the differences in their underlying paradigms or worldviews. I tried synthesizing ideas without first having a basic functional, insider's understanding of Chinese culture in general and Chinese martial arts culture specifically. As a result, I wound up with a confused stew pot of ideas. I learned to "talk the talk" of the internal martial arts and in doing so, fooled myself into believing that I actually knew something. This presented a huge obstacle to making demonstrable progress.

Eventually I sorted it all out. Here's my understanding as of this writing. Let's start with some basic definitions.

What is a paradigm? The Merriam-Webster Online dictionary defines paradigm as:

> a philosophical and theoretical framework of a scientific school or discipline within which theories, laws, and generalizations and the experiments performed in support of them are formulated; broadly : a philosophical or theoretical framework of any kind

What is a worldview? The Merriam-Webster Online dictionary defines worldview as "a comprehensive conception or apprehension of the world especially from a specific standpoint"

Note: *worldview* is the English translation of the German philosophical term, *weltanschauung*.

What is culture? The Merriam-Webster Online dictionary defines *culture* as:

> the customary beliefs, social forms, and material traits of a racial, religious, or social group; also: the characteristic features of everyday existence (as diversions or a way of life) shared by people in a place or time

What do paradigm, worldview, and culture have to do with internal martial arts and this book? In a word, everything!

As you know, the physical technologies of Tai-chi, Ba-gua, and Xing-yi originated in China and Aikido originated in Japan. These cultures, like our Western, American culture, each have a unique culture, paradigm, and worldview. Learning each of these physical technologies in the U.S. is often accompanied by learning terminology and concepts from the culture, paradigm, or worldview in which they originated.

Learning another culture is fine, however, there is little in common between 'western' and 'eastern' culture when it comes to those aspects typically associated with the internal martial arts. Here, I am particularly referring to the Chinese term "Qi" and the Japanese term "Ki" and the Indian term "Prana". If western civilization had retained and maintained the concept of *aer* as established by the ancient Greek philosopher, Anaximenes of Miletus (circa 545 BCE), then we might have a bridge to understanding "Qi", "Ki" and "Prana". But we don't.

The bottom line is that the typical English translations of "Qi" and "Ki" as *energy* or *life force* do not provide a functional understanding of how these terms are used in the internal martial arts. I've recently learned that *Qi flowing* is a short-hand way of noting that a particular kinesthetic quality has been achieved. Also, *sinking the Qi* refers to a particular kinesthetic phenomenon. Neither of these physical qualities has anything to do with the typical translation and popular understanding.

And this is where and how I got stuck for many years. I didn't make real progress until after I was able to let go of my attachment to the concept of "Qi" and focused on developing functional physical skillsets. And so, the ideas I share in this book are presented using the American, or western paradigm, worldview, and culture. Speaking in our common vernacular provides the clearest communication on a difficult subject.

Also, keep in mind that the original founders and family lineage practitioners worked within their range of understanding of human body biomechanics. If we can apply recent advances in understanding of biomechanics and fascia research by sports medicine, exercise physiologists, physical therapists, etc., then we stand to make real and lasting contributions to these arts. But we can only do this when we let go of the notion that somehow, functional progress is co-achieved through facility with alien words, concepts and philosophies rooted in a distant past.

What I am discovering as I develop these physical skillsets is that I am able to kind of reverse-translate a feeling-skillset into the words and concepts of the original writings. For example, when I feel "x" I get an insight into what I think "y" is trying to describe. This I believe is the more functional way to understand the original culture and writings of the internal martial arts. The dysfunctional way, which is the road I originally followed, is to first intellectually understand the words and concepts and then try to imagine the feeling that I think is being expressed. The latter route led me to a dead end. How's it working for you?

3

Wujifa: The Way of Connection

Wujifa (pronounced, *woo jee fah*) is philosophically based on the Chinese concept of Wuji or Wu-chi (無 極;wú jí), the undifferentiated state that existed prior to Yin-Yang, Taiji and the ten thousand things. Wujifa takes a different approach to understanding Wuji, the state before divisions and separations, by considering Wuji as the original state where everything is connected. To return to the Tao then means to re-connect, to return to a condition of connectedness. According to http://wujifa.com/

Wujifa is the practice of developing depth and understanding of subtle connections. These connections are often functionally explored in the training of body and mind through various practices.

One of the keys to the practice of Wujifa is developing a unique form of relaxed strength that involves working with fascial pathways, what we often simply call developing connections.

When one understands how to utilize the connective tissues, one steps through the door and starts to understand what is meant by internal movement in the practice of Wujifa.

The "fa" (法;fǎ) in Wujifa uses a less common understanding of "fa" as *principle*. The typical translation is: law, method, way. So literally, Wujifa means, the way of connection; the principle of connection. And for those living in a disconnected, disassociated state, Wujifa provides a way to develop internal connectedness which is experienced as that elusive and unique kinesthetic quality known as internal strength.

4

Visualization, Feeling and Tucking Under

A lot of teaching in these kinesthetic arts is "monkey-see-monkey-do". Many students who later become teachers will pass on what they were taught without comparing, questioning and analyzing what they were taught against the principles underlying the arts they were learning. I went down this road myself.

There are many levels of feeling. Some people say that if you do the forms or exercises correctly, then you will "feel the Qi". This may be true but you will only feel to the level of feeling you are currently capable of feeling. This is one of those obvious truths that are frequently overlooked. While it is good practice to follow the feeling that a teacher may elicit in your body, bear in mind that whatever you feel is only what you are currently capable of feeling. There is much, much more.

Since this is a book about the pelvis, let's look at some examples of levels of feeling in the pelvis. A level of feeling that you are probably most familiar with is the feeling of your muscles engaging when you stop a stream of urine or you squeeze to prevent wind or defecation. You may feel a fullness above your pubic bone when your bladder is really, really full. You may also feel muscles engaging when you perform various exercises involving the pelvic muscles. Feeling at the muscle-level is a good functional first step.

Going deeper, feeling the intention, the feeling just before the muscles fully contract to demonstrate an externally observable movement, is another level of feeling.

Going deeper, feeling the fascial stretch during an exercise and not knowing how it showed up is another level of feeling.

Many teachers prefer to use "visualization" or "imagery" as a method for driving intention. The problem with this is that visualization and imagery interject a component of imagination between intention and the muscle firing. When I was not aware of this subtlety, I got lost in the imagination process. My chronic muscle tensions and fascial adhesions prevented my body from responding to my imagined intention. Because I could not feel into my tensions and stuck areas, I did not know that my body was not responding. As a result, I erroneously believed I was doing what I imagined or visualized I was doing. This, I discovered is the danger or illusion of using visualization or imagery.

One problem I had as a new student with "tucking under" is that I interpreted this as a rule and I approached the task very rigidly; tuck and lock. This was absolutely wrong. The point is not to *lock* the lumbar in a straight line but to *unlock* the lumbo-sacral area so this part of the body can respond dynamically and functionally according to the situation.

If I were to say that there is a danger in tucking the tailbone, the danger is that this can be interpreted as "the secret" for those hungry for secret powers; as when I was hungry for that secret power. It wound up being a place where I got stuck and locked-in.

Relax the back. Relax the front. Find a relaxed homeostatic position somewhere between an extreme arch and extreme tuck. Relax. Drop the tailbone.

When the practitioner lets go of holding in the chest and the pelvis is properly adjusted, the practitioner experiences his/her thighs as feeling like they're carrying more weight than normally. Relaxing the muscles that hold the arch in the back reduces the 'energetic' blockage to 'dropping the weight'.

Breathing, by design, involves the whole body. However, I had learned to tighten here and tighten there and so I restricted my breathing. The elasticity of the pelvis and the pelvic floor is part of the breathing process. Forcing a "tuck" hampers breathing.

5

Relaxing the Waist and Abdominal Breathing

A typical instruction in the internal martial arts is to relax the chest and breathe from the belly. In my early days, it took me a long time to learn how to expand and contract the space between my navel and rib cage. This to me became the definition of abdominal- or belly-breathing. Later, when I got into Wujifa, I was told to breathe deeper. And so I worked on pushing my belly out further. "No! Breathe lower. Allow the abdomen to expand all the way down to the pubic bone." Wow! I couldn't do that.... then... but now... I can. Here's what I've learned.

The Inner Body site has a really nice graphic of the abdomen. Go check it out and then come back.
http://www.innerbody.com/anatomy/muscular/lower-torso-male

Notice the lower half of the lower section of the rectus abdominus muscle is about where you find the upper border of the fascia of the External abdominal oblique muscles. This is typically the area between the navel and the pubic bone. About two-thirds of this area looks like it's the fascia of the external abdominal oblique muscles and about a third looks like it's the muscle of the rectus abdominus. Simply relaxing the rectus abdominus, the front of the belly, will not get movement in this lower area if the muscle groups to both sides of the rectus abdominus are tense. To get movement in the belly all the way down to the pubic bone requires the lower muscle strands of the external obliques to relax. The waist must relax.

But wait, there's more. Underneath the external abdominal oblique muscles are the internal abdominal oblique muscles which run perpendicular to the external obliques. And under these are the transverse abdominus muscles! Three layers of muscles to relax and let go! Where do you begin?

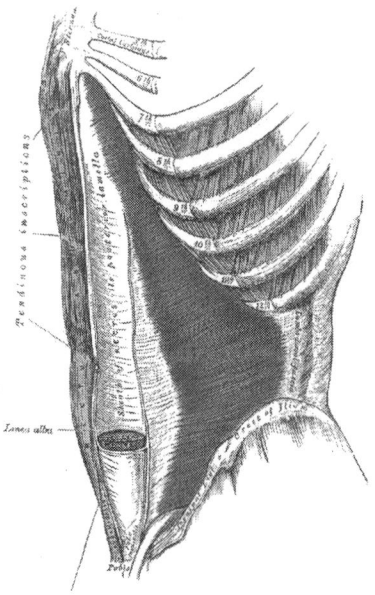

http://en.wikipedia.org/wiki/File:Transversus_abdominis.png

The good news was that I didn't have to figure out how to relax each individual muscle group. All I had to do was figure out how to get the area immediately above the pubic bone to relax and move. Enter the role of intention and practice. What I discovered is that movement in this area is a kind of bio-feedback device of the various muscles groups that make up "the waist" relaxing! Or said another way, a measure of the waist relaxing may be found in the degree to which you are able to observe and feel the area immediately above the pubic bone expanding and contracting with your breathing. This took me years to figure out.

Based on my current understanding, I think this is a very functional way to approach the admonition to "relax the waist".

6

Introducing the Crotch, Waist, and Hips

Over the years, I've read hundreds of books, magazines and journal articles and watched countless movies and videos. But it wasn't until I started finding references to the crotch, waist, and hips for this book that I realized that I'd seen some of these excerpts before. How could I have missed or not deeply investigated such important points!? Given the way I've approached learning (amassing data), I'm certain that I glossed over these important elements as I tried to conceptually understand all the data of the entire book, article or training video without thoroughly grasping each point and pursuing it deeply before moving on to the next section of the book, article or video.

And so when I began the journey of writing this book, I thought that a good place to start would be to gather together as many excerpts referencing the crotch, waist, and hips that I could find that were written by martial artists. By putting these all in one place, that is by isolating these references and making them the central focus or theme of a book, really got me thinking about this topic. For me, the end result of this project has been a heightened awareness of the importance that each of these authors express about the pelvis. I hope you find this to be true too.

Here are a few samples, both in English and Chinese from the longer list of excerpts in both English and Chinese that I complied in Appendix A: References to Crotch, Waist, and Hips in Martial Arts.

Distinguishing the Hip and Waist by Sam Masich.
http://www.embracethemoon.com/perspectives/hip_waist.htm

There is perhaps, no greater stumbling block to the mastery of Taijiquan, than the murky confusion we are greeted with when we first begin a conscious study of the hips and waist. Virtually nothing in our western physical education prepares us for the study of this region.

Combat Techniques of Taiji, Xingyi, and Bagua: Principles and Practices of Internal Martial Arts. (2006). Lu Shengli and Zhang Yun. pg. 137-139.

Song yao – relax the waist: *Song yao* is one of the most important key points because it involves your waist, which is the center of your body and the locus of control for all your movements. If your waist is tight, you will not be able to relax any other part of your body. Your qi will not be able to move smoothly throughout your body, your internal force will not be sustained, your arms will not be flexible, and your footwork will not be nimble.

Guo dang – curve and expand the crotch: In *guo dang*, the arch formed by the inside surfaces of your legs and your crotch should expand and maintain a curved shape. This will help your *qi* sink and move smoothly down to your legs without becoming dissipated. *Guo dang* will also increase your root and the power in your legs. It will make your whole body very nimble.

Liu tun – tuck the buttocks under the lower back: *Liu tun* means that you must keep your lower spine straight so that your buttocks do not protrude. This movement will allow your waist to remain relaxed and your *shen* to rise.

The Essential Training and Coordination of the Waist and Hips in Chen Style Tai Chi Chuan Practice
(腰部和臀部的基本训练和协调的陈式太极拳练习)

by Chen En, Sports Science Research, 2002-01, pg. 71-86.
http://en.cnki.com.cn/Article_en/CJFDTOTAL-TYKY200201021.htm

同时还应与腰部密切配合，塌腰时需含裆，活腰时需松裆，而拧腰发劲时需扣裆，这样上下盘才易合，内劲在周身各处才能沉着透达。

The waist and crotch should be closely coordinated. Relaxing the waist helps keep the crotch relaxed. When the waist is alive and the crotch is relaxed, when twisting the waist as in fa-jin, you need to draw in the crotch. When the waist and crotch are relaxed, then the top and bottom "plates" are easier to fit together (like stacking dishes). Internal strength is attained when the whole body is calm.

Using Crotch Techniques (运裆之技法) by Lin QuanBao or Lim Chuan Poh (林泉宝). 2007-08-06.
http://blog.sina.com.cn/s/blog_48b6934401000b1c.html

练太极拳功夫主要的就是练"裆"。

The main practice of Tai-chi Chuan gongfu is training the "crotch".

太极拳活与不活，全在于裆的运作。裆不活，动作必然呆滞。裆胯是太极拳的天机。所谓"天机"者，玄机关窍之意，凡动作变化全凭于此。不得此中奥秘，难以练成太极功夫。

Whether Tai-Chi Chuan is alive or not depends on the full operation of the crotch. If the crotch is not alive, then movement will inevitably be sluggish. The crotch and hip is the secret of Tai-chi Chuan. This so-called "secret", means every change in action depends on this mysterious body opening. Without understanding this profound mystery, it is hard to imagine succeeding in training Tai-chi gongfu.

7

Qigong or Not Qigong

I would be remiss to not include a section about qigong even though I am not a self-avowed qigong practitioner. Many people recognize zhan zhuang as the "King of Qigong" and some even refer to Tai-chi as a form of qigong. While I do practice both zhan zhuang and Taijiquan, I do not consider either of these practices to be qigong. Why? Because I'm not focusing on feeling or moving my qi.

In my early Tai-chi days, I had read about and attended seminars on qigong. I visualized and imagined my "qi flowing". As it turned out, I could not have been more misguided. Many years later and still perplexed by this whole "qi thing", I did some research and stumbled upon a book titled: Qigong Fever: Body, Science and Utopia in China by David Palmer (2007). I highly recommend this book to anyone who either is currently or is considering practicing qigong! After reading this and thinking about when and how qigong entered mainstream America, my understanding is that "qigong" was appropriated by the New Age leaders in the U.S. during the height of the qigong craze in China and was repackaged as a kind of dissociated, mystified, mind-body practice for a mass consumer culture.

In my experience qigong teachers jump too quickly to "feeling your qi between your hands" and encouraging visualizing qi flowing without first guiding students through the months or years of relaxing their bodies and helping them develop a functional sense of feeling ever more subtle levels of feeling. Without this basic work of integration, the mind-body disassociation is maintained. As I've learned, the work of getting students to relax, let go, and develop the ability to feel ever more subtle levels of kinesthetic feelings cannot be accomplished when students attend class to be entertained or to get more stuff to pack into their bag of experiences or to be able to say, "Look! I learned qigong!"

Nonetheless, for the purpose of this book, I include excerpts from books and articles on qigong that reference the pelvic area as yet another example of the importance of being able to relax, feel, and gain some level of control of this area of the body.

See Appendix B: Qigong – Excerpts from Books and Articles in English.

8

Internal Strength – Whole-body Connectedness

In my opinion, there are many who think they've got these highest levels of whole-body connectedness and teach their level of understanding as if that level were the highest level but in fact there are few people who actually have these highest levels of whole-body connectedness. The folks who think they have it but don't are doing a disservice to their students and the internal martial arts community. To me, it would serve everyone better if the teacher were to honestly say, "This is not it but this is all I know now. I can only take you this far." But alas, that perspective doesn't fill classrooms and seminars nor sell books and videos.

So, here is my understanding based on where I am as of this writing, meaning, what I am developing an ability to see and discern what looks like whole-body movement vs. movement that despite being highly coordinated, still lacks that certain quality of deeper internal connectedness.

Beginning, intermediate, and advanced students as well as some long-established teachers have never developed this skill, nor have they trained with those who had this skill. I say this based on my knowledge of the history of internal martial arts in the United States. As such, speculation and misunderstanding abound when these practitioners say, "This is what internal strength is."

I disagree with those who say that you must get your hands on someone who truly has internal skills to feel what they are doing because it is not visible in videos. It is not sufficient to visit someone who is said to have skill because the fact is that you can only "see" to your current level of skill and feeling-ability. Also, someone's skill *is* plainly visible in videos *after* you have developed a higher level of skill in your own body. I have discovered that I can only see in others what I have changed-away-from, through training my body, or what has been repeatedly pointed out to me by those who have changed even more. This I know to be true from my own experience.

Exercises to develop these skills can vary stylistically and according to the personal preferences of the instructor. This in itself is not the problem. The question is whether these exercises yield functional results. In Wujifa, training focuses on developing fascial connectedness. Moving with fascial connectedness and being able to move in a relaxed manner while maintaining ground path connection is considered internal strength. This kinesthetic quality is radically different from bracing which many consider to be internal strength.

Here's an excerpt from Running Times which illustrates the increasing acknowledgement of the role of fascia. To my knowledge, the internal martial arts community has yet to grasp the significance of this.

Understanding Your Fascia. (June 10, 2011). Julia Lucas. http://runningtimes.com/Article.aspx?ArticleID=23045&PageNum=2

Under your skin, encasing your body and webbing its way through your insides like spider webs, is fascia. Fascia is made up primarily of densely packed collagen fibers that create a full body system of sheets, chords and bags that wrap, divide and permeate every one of your muscles, bones, nerves, blood vessels and organs. Every bit of you is encased in it. You're protected by fascia, connected by fascia and kept in taut human shape by fascia.

In 2007 the first international Fascia Research Congress, held at Harvard Medical School, brought about a new demand for attention to the fascial system.

While you may not share the medical and bodywork communities' excitement over mechanotransduction and the contractile properties of myofibroblasts, think of it this way: Fascia is a major player in every movement you make and every injury you've ever had, but until five years ago nobody paid it any attention. And now they're making up for lost time.

What rocked the medical community's world was this: Fascia isn't just plastic wrap. Fascia can contract and feel and impact the way you move. It's our richest sense organ, it possesses the ability to contract independently of the muscles it surrounds and it responds to stress without your conscious command. That's a big deal.

Unfortunately, it's very unlikely that your fascia maintains its optimal flexibility, shape or texture. Lack of activity will cement the once-supple fibers into place. Chronic stress causes the fibers to thicken in an attempt to protect the underlying muscle. Poor posture and lack of flexibility and repetitive movements pull the fascia into ingrained patterns. Adhesions form within the stuck and damaged fibers like snags in a sweater, and once they've formed they're hard to get rid of.

So what does moving with fascial connectedness look like to me? Picture a scuba diver wearing a full wet-suit. Or picture Spiderman wearing his colorful spandex suit. Picture either of these folks now extending an arm or making any other movement. The movement stretches and pulls the suit far past the joint which is moving. Moving with fascial connection kind of looks like a moving flexible exo-skeleton, like a wet-suit or a spandex suit.

Here's something you can try that should make this clear to you. Go to your bed. Make sure the bed has a sheet (what you sleep on top of) and a cover sheet over that (what you sleep under), and a blanket on top of the cover sheet. (Use cotton sheets and not silk or satin because cotton provides the right amount of friction needed for this model to work.) With nothing else on the bed, smooth and tighten the sheets and blanket. Do not tuck-in or anchor the cover sheet and blanket; leave it spread smoothly over the bottom sheet. Now, standing or kneeling at one side of the bed and with one hand, grab an edge of the cover sheet (that is under the blanket) and give this a series of soft, gentle pulls. What do you notice? The energy you exert is transmitted across the bed moving the blanket somewhat evenly on a path from your hand to the side opposite you.

Now, take a 5 pound/2 kg weight and place this on the bed at a half arm's length in front of you. Exert the same level of soft, gentle pull. What do you notice? The movement stops at the weight. To get the weight to move you have to exert more force. Now replace the 5 pound/2 kg weight with a 10 pound/4.5kg weight. Exert the same soft gentle pull you did the first time. What do you notice? How much more force do you need to exert to move that 10 pound/4.5 kg weight?

As you may have guessed, the cover sheet you are pulling represents your underlying connective tissue, your fascial chain, and the blanket represents your skin and each weight represents a physical injury or emotionally traumatic event; a place where there is a chronic muscular tension, a muscle fibrosis (knot, spasm, scar tissue), or a fascial adhesion. Depending on your age and life experiences, you may have several differently sized weights on the bed. The heavier weights represent the more deeply ingrained blockages and thus those that are the more deeply inhibitive to free connected movement.

Now, take this experience as a model and watch how internal martial arts practitioners and teachers move. Where do you see their "weight" breaking the free flow of movement through their body? Where are they stuck? Where is the muscle knot, holding, fascial adhesion? Where are you stuck? In the "Qi" paradigm, the free flow would be called "Qi flowing" and where weights block the free movement would be called "Qi not flowing". It's pretty simple but really hard to do.

Another model that is also typically referenced is the tensional integrity - tensegrity - structure. These have been used to describe the fascial system. You can find various videos on the internet describing tensegrity structures. After watching these, if you were to conceptually layer the bed sheet model over a tensegrity structure, I think this is about as close to modeling whole-body connected human movement outside of the human body as is possible at this time.

Obviously, the human body is much more complex than the tensegrity or bed sheet models. There are multiple fascial pathways twining through multiple layers of connective tissue. So please keep in mind that these examples are over-simplifications! This is the best I can describe how internal movement / internal strength looks and feels to me at this point. I can't move this way yet. When I try to distinguish those who move in this manner from those who don't, I don't always get it right. I'm seeing partly through body training and partly through conceptual training. I'm not yet seeing purely through the experience of personal kinesthetic skillsets.

Here are a couple videos about fascia that I really like. Go watch these now and come back.

Fascia and stretching: The Fuzz Speech. (Feb 7, 2009).
Gil Hedley, Ph.D.
http://www.youtube.com/watch?v=_FtSP-tkSug

Gil Hedley Reconsidering "The Fuzz" Part 2. (April 7, 2012).
Gil Hedley, Ph.D.
Presentation at the 2012 International Fascial Congress
http://www.youtube.com/watch?v=D0LlR7Bq0So

Fascia - architecture of connective tissue. (January 15, 2011)
http://www.youtube.com/watch?v=rGzM6rpS4j8
Dr. Tom Findley summarizes a 1988 Ph.D. thesis, The Architecture of Connective Tissue in the Musculoskeletal System by Japp Van der Wal, M.D., Ph.D.

9

Comfort Level 1: Basic Data about Your Pelvis

*The pelvis is the key to man's well-being,
as wise men have taught from time immemorial... - Dr. Ida Rolf*

If you're like me, you probably grew up knowing nothing of your "privates" outside of habits developed in childhood toilet training, to learning this was a vulnerable area to protect in a hostile situation, to your experiences with puberty and adult sexual activity. And even if you did take a human anatomy and physiology class along the way and try to relate this information to your internal martial arts practice, it is still likely that you have a gap in your experience and understanding of your pelvis and its role in your practice.

Throughout my first twenty years of Tai-chi, Bagua, and Xing-yi classes, I never heard any teacher talk about the pelvis, except maybe to "tuck", "belly breathe", "round the crotch" or move from the dan-tian. When it was first suggested to me that I work on relaxing my pelvic floor, first, I didn't know what this was and when it was explained to me, I recoiled in disgust at the thought of what was being proposed. I was stuck. It took me a more than a year to simply get comfortable with the mere idea that it is O.K. to work on relaxing this part of my own body before I actually began doing anything! For me as a male, a book that helped me approach the conceptual hurdle was, Out in the Open: The Complete Male Pelvis by R. Louis Schultz, Ph.D. (1999). I learned a lot about my own body in relation to culture, overall physicality, emotions, stages of the male life-span and more that I had never before considered.

From my experience, the pelvis in general, and the pelvic floor or crotch specifically, is the most *not-talked-about* part of the body in the internal martial arts and yet from everything I've heard and read, it is the key area for generating powerful internal movement! The closest that most typical internal martial art "talk" gets to talking about the pelvis is by way of mentioning the dan-tian which is typically referenced as being 2" - 3" below the navel. Why not refer to the dan-tian as being 2" - 3" above the pubic bone or midway between the navel and pubic bone? Is the choice of the navel as a point of reference (rather than the pubic bone) an insignificant detail that can be ignored or is this an indication of a social or cultural taboo at work? I suggest that it is the latter. Another aspect of this book is to address these social or cultural taboos straight on.

In my early days of learning the internal martial arts, I was taught to use my mind to move my Qi (the Yi leads the Qi). But what I wasn't aware of was that my body was rigid with chronic tension (even though I could wiggle like a noodle). No amount of Yi was going to move any Qi through this locked-down structure! And of course, this method yielded no result! If anything, this approach only re-enforced my mind-body disassociation.

Taking a functional approach, learning about the muscles and muscle groups I need to work on provided me a way to become aware of, familiar with, and remain grounded in my body. While knowing the names and function of muscles does not in itself contribute to the work of feeling and relaxing these muscles, knowing the terminology and function does help me connect with myself as well as understand what the massage and physical therapists have to contribute to the conversation. And when I am told to work on relaxing specific muscles or muscle groups, I know what I am targeting. There are palpable, tangible steps that can result in demonstrable results.

For this next section I've done a fair amount of reading research to learn about the role of the muscles of the pelvis as well as how they connect to the rest of the body. There are many illustrations that appear in books and journals which I'd love to include here but for the first edition of this book, I have not requested permissions. If you are interested, I urge you to go to these articles cited in the References and see these illustrations yourself.

Since I could not find any western, clinical-type research regarding how the pelvis is used in the internal martial arts, this section pulls together excerpts from various sources which I believe are related enough to my personal experiences to contribute to helping me reach a fuller understanding of the core, the center, the pelvis.

A typical short description of the pelvis goes something like this: The pelvis consists of three bones, the sacrum (the bottom end of the spine) and an ilium on either side. These three bones are held together at their joints by very strong ligaments. The muscles of the torso and legs anchor on the pelvis. The round cavity in the center of the pelvis is where the muscles of the pelvic floor attach. In our normal upright position, the weight of our internal organs largely rest on the pelvic floor muscles. The pelvic floor muscles have long been associated with childbirth and/or incontinence but are more recently being recognized as contributing to stabilizing the pelvic girdle.

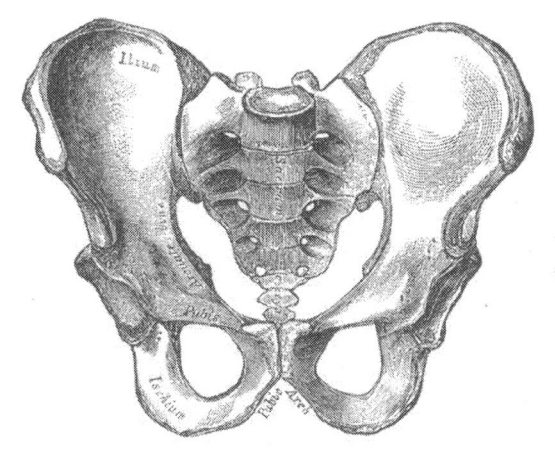

http://en.wikipedia.org/wiki/File:Gray241.png

The problem for me with this kind of quick-and-to-the-point description is that it is really easy for me to gloss over and move to the next bit of information and dismiss the importance of what I just read. It's too easy to miss all the intricacies that have been abstracted or summarized. And so for this reason, I've provided a longer, yet selected, list of information that I discovered while writing this book. Really! I didn't know any of this before. And so this list represents the extent of my understanding at this time. Sources for this list can be found in the

Secrets of the Pelvis for Martial Arts

References section. Take your time reading this list. Consider the implications of each item to your training. Notice what you become aware of as you read.

Twenty-Three Things to Know About Your Pelvis

1. The pelvis or pelvic ring is comprised of three bones: the sacrum and two innominate. The innominate are the two side bones which consist of three parts: ilium, ischium, and pubis. These three bones (ilium, ischium, and pubis) fully ossify and fuse into one bone by age 20-25.

2. The primary function of the pelvis is to support the weight of the torso which constitutes about 2/3 of the weight of the body as well as loads applied to it.

3. The wedge shaped sacrum is the keystone of the "arch bridge" of the pelvis. The sacrum is the foundation of the spine.

4. The sacrum "floats" in-between the two innominate and is held in place by ligaments. There is no specific "groove" in which it sets. Therefore, the sacrum can move up, down, forward, backward depending on the forces acting upon it. The forward and backward rotation of the sacrum can be 2-4 millimeters. (Another source says up to 4" though movement of 2" or less is normal.)

5. The sacrum may remain freely moveable over the age of 80. However, a limited range of daily movement habits can cause "fixation" in the sacro-iliac joint which further inhibits motion and reduces optimal pelvic performance. Movement may lessen with age.

6. The base of the sacrum naturally moves backward (and the top moves forward) when standing and vice versa when sitting.

7. Forty-five muscles attach to the pelvis and some of these are the largest muscles in the body. If any of these muscles are shortened,

spastic, and/or not in balance with all other muscles, these imbalances can distort pelvic mechanics. Relaxed, supple, muscular balance provides optimal pelvic performance and transfer of loads or forces.

8. If the pelvic floor muscles are too tight, they can pull the sacrum out of alignment which can affect the efficient transfer of forces to and from the torso. Alignment of the pelvis affects body performance.

9. When the rear ligaments of the sacro-iliac joint shorten, they tend to push the base of the sacrum forward into the pelvic basin. When the front sacro-iliac joint ligaments shorten, the sacral base tends to "bulge" out the back.

10. Pelvic floor muscles that are already tight will appear weak in a squeeze test because there is not much difference between the rest state and tightened state. That said, there is no agreed upon standard to determine if the pelvic floor is performing correctly or not.

11. Pelvic floor problems are more often caused by habitual movement patterns and less often by a one-time traumatic event.

12. Sucking in the abdomen creates an upward internal force which pulls the contents of the abdomen as well as the pelvic floor upward toward the diaphragm. This restricts full, natural movement.

13. Muscles respond to the position or activity in which we spend most of our time.

14. The body's natural ability to compensate can hide the original problem and mask symptoms, for example, of misaligned pelvic joints. You may not know that you have a 'sub-clinical' spasm. Because connective tissue (fascia) connects the entire body, a tight or spastic muscle in one area can "show up" in another area. Eventually, seemingly unrelated problems may arise due to fatigue of the compensatory mechanism.

15. Tense pelvic floor muscles have the capacity to cause a backward rotation of the sacrum. Since the sacrum is the pelvis' load-bearing bone for the spine, a less than optimal alignment would decrease the efficiency of torso load transfer to ground.

16. The connection between the pelvic floor muscles and the legs is found in the obturator internus muscle whose fascia provides an origination for the levator ani muscle.

17. The "pelvic core" is comprised of the pelvic floor on the bottom, the respiratory diaphragm on top, the abdominals in front and paraspinals in back. These muscles work together synergistically to create intra-abdominal pressure.

18. The muscles of the pelvic floor, the transversus abdominus in front and the multifidus muscles along the spine co-contract; they all "fire" together. And so, tension in the abdomen co-exists with tension in the pelvic floor.

19. The pelvic floor moves in sync with the diaphragm when breathing. On inhale, the distance between the top crest of the ilium narrows and the lower part widens with the release of the pelvic floor and the lumbar spine lengthens. On exhale, the pelvic floor tightens, the lower part of the pelvis narrows, the top widens, and the lumbar spine returns to its curve.

20. Kegels and the yoga posture "mula bandha" (which involves contracting and lifting the perineum), are under-taught and often misunderstood which can lead to more problems.

21. In a normal standing posture, the line of gravity passes posterior to the hip joint but anterior to the sacrum.

22. The muscles and organs of the pelvic floor are innervated by the pudendal nerve which emerges from S2-S4 on both sides of the sacrum and branches into three sections; one branch goes to the anal-

rectal area, another goes to the perineum, and another goes to the genitals.

23. Even though the pelvic floor muscles are enervated from separate left and right nerve branches, they function as a single unit instead of contracting individually.

Why would I think this list is important for internal martial arts practice? Does knowing any of this help you feel a functional connectedness through your body? Maybe as you read this list you became a little more aware of your pelvic area. Maybe you began to wonder if you could feel some of the aspects about which you were reading. Can you feel your pelvic floor move with your breath? At the very least, if this short list helped you develop a more detailed understanding of the role your pelvic area plays in posture, movement, and receiving and expressing force, then it has served its purpose.

Here are a few videos that fit nicely in right here. You may want to take a little time and view these.

1. **Pelvic Floor Demystified.** (June 10, 2010). Katy Bowman http://www.youtube.com/watch?v=IOoTC9DpB3k (Total time 5:08)
   <Note: This is such an excellent and succinct explanation you have to go watch this now! >

2. **SI Joint Anatomy, Biomechanics & Prevalence.** (Nov 29, 2011) http://www.youtube.com/watch?v=D6NTMgWCSaU (Total time 3:10)

3. **Pelvic Floor Part 1 - The Pelvic Diaphragm - 3D Anatomy Tutorial.** (Feb 2, 2013). anatomyzone.com http://www.youtube.com/watch?v=P3BBAMWm2Eo (Total time: 10:27)

4. **Pelvic Anatomy Sacro-iliac Joint physical therapy animations.** (Apr 26, 2011). MediLaw.TV

http://www.youtube.com/watch?v=xxktB0kqIeY

5. **10 step guide to pelvic floor safe exercise**
   http://www.pelvicfloorfirst.org.au/pages/how-can-i-make-my-program-pelvic-floor-safe.html

6. **Hip and Lower Back Pain Exercises**. Dr. Laura Fields
   http://spinecarefitness.com/hip-and-lower-back-pain-exercises

A couple "apps" currently available and which can show much greater detail of musculature than these old Gray's Anatomy drawings are: "Visible Human Body" and "Virtual Human Body". Also, an internet search on: pelvic floor muscles will yield a wide variety of very good, contemporary illustrations. There are also many websites that provide wonderfully detailed anatomical descriptions. What I provide here should be considered a basic introduction.

10

Identifying Chronic Tension

Developing internal strength for the internal martial arts involves identifying chronic tension or holding patterns and then relaxing these or letting these go. However, chronic tension is hidden from me. My body is to me just what it is. In reality, there is no distinction between "my" and "body". And yet, in our English language we routinely say, "My body" as if "I" were the separate and distinct owner of a "body". This is one pretty obvious example of the extent to which our mind-body disassociation is linguistically and culturally embedded.

I don't experience my body as being chronically tense and yet it is. Consider these examples that showed up in me during some early Wujifa zhan zhuang classes:

- My head tilts slightly to one side. Adjusting it to vertical makes it feel like it is tilting.
- I sometimes lean forward. Adjusting my torso to vertical makes it feel like I'm tilting backward.
- Adjusting the right side of the pelvis results in the left shoulder moving.
- Most often, my pelvis just doesn't adjust in the direction being suggested.
- The admonition to allow myself to relax results in my relaxing to the limits of that which I can allow myself to relax. I can't relax what I can't feel. What I can't feel is usually what is chronically tense.

I liken the earlier Wujifa classes I attended to Michelangelo trying to carve the David with only a butter knife where my instructor was Michelangelo and I was the block of granite! My musculature was so rigid that my teacher's adjustments to my posture were nearly impossible! Things have improved over the years but the further I go, the further I see I need to go.

Here's another example. I may think my shoulders are relaxed. I may even feel they are relaxed given my current level of feeling-ability which is my benchmark of what relaxed is for me. However, when a finger or massage tool presses into a tense muscle, I yelp in pain and pull away. This experience, though not necessarily pleasant, has helped me notice a tense area and where I need to work on relaxing. Sometimes a tense muscle carries more of an emotional charge; pressing into the muscle is not as physically painful as it is emotionally distressing.

All these experiences led me to conclude that: chronic muscular tension is invisible to me until it is brought to my conscious awareness, that is, until it is physically pointed out to me!

The Importance of Scar Tissue Release Therapy in <u>Massage Today</u> (June, 2009, Vol. 09, Issue 06). Marjorie Brook, LMT, CIMI

Scar tissue therapy is generally overlooked by health professionals because the extent of physiological effects scars can have on the body have never really been acknowledged.

A simple scar from a childhood accident to major surgery can have a lifelong effect both physically and mentally for your client. Scar tissue has the potential to spread in any direction including internally throughout the body. It can also restrict movement or function anywhere in the body from a joint to an organ.

While not every scar presents a problem, often they can. This is due to the fact that the body is one large, three-dimensional piece of fascia that envelops us like an intricate spider web. Any kink, pull or restriction in one area affects the whole matrix.

This is why I think that for beginner and even intermediate practitioners, the "breathe, contract and relax" methods of relaxing are ineffective for identifying and addressing underlying chronic tensions. There is no substitute for manually pushing into muscles or having someone try to make adjustments to your posture to identify where the tensions are located! And for someone like me who gave my body a beating in my youth, I've got my share of scar tissue to work through! I hear about this every time I go for Rolfing massage, "Mike, you sure have a lot of scar tissue in your ankles!"

Well, what about stretching? In my own experience, I have found dissymmetry in my body when doing certain physical therapy or yoga-like postures; one limb has less movement than its companion. Sometimes stretching can help to restore a fuller range of motion. However, I cannot feel into those areas of muscular scar tissue, knots, spasms, tension; those areas where I am holding, or those areas where I am "frozen". And so when I stretch what happens is that where I am frozen in one area, I become hyperflexible in another. It's as if what can stretch, will stretch, and what cannot, does not. I've discovered that stretching alone cannot dissolve scar tissue, spasms, knots, holding patterns. Stretching for this purpose can be an illusory dead end.

Pelvic Power: Mind/Body Exercises for Strength, Flexibility, Posture, and Balance for Men and Women (2003), by Eric Franklin

...the female pelvic floor is more flexible; the male floor tends to be less flexible... Thus the training program has predetermined goals: increased flexibility for men, and building up of strength for women. (pg. xi)

Exercising a certain area of the body is not the same as experiencing its function in daily life. If one can realize that the pelvic floor supports almost every movement we make, this in itself is a very effective training. But this can only be realized when one feels how the pelvic floor is involved in our movement. (pg. 2)

So if I can't feel where I am tense or holding, then how can I know if that muscle, muscle group, or kinetic chain is functioning correctly or not? If my movement is hampered by tension or holding somewhere in the system, then I will not have a clean path for my intention to connect through. Tension blocks intention.

Structure of a Skeletal Muscle

http://en.wikipedia.org/wiki/File:Illu_muscle_structure.jpg

William Zmachinsky, at the Prostrate Massage and Health site, describes the problem that I encounter every day in my job. http://www.prostate-massage-and-health.com/Anal-peripheral-prostate-massage.html

> When you sit all day long, you constrict the blood flow to your anal area. Not only is it being pinched off in the lower abdomen, you have the weight of your entire upper body pushing down on your anal area. You are actually suffocating it!

> The blood flow is greatly diminished and the nerve energy is diminished. The lack of blood, oxygen and nutrients actually cause the muscles to stiffen and get hard. In Neuro-Muscular Therapy (NMT)

they call this hard muscle tissue "Schemic Tissue". It is not hard like an athlete's muscles. It is hard like dead muscle!

When adults worry or stress out a lot, they often constrict these same muscles without even being aware of it! When your anal muscles are tight, your blood flow is reduced.

Here are a few more excerpts of a longer article that points to how tension in the muscles that anchor to the pelvis can cause the pelvis to go out of alignment.

Who Cares About Pelvic Alignment? Dr. Sue Ironside. http://www.ultrafitness.net/pelvic%20alignment.pdf

As runners, we tend to be aware of our muscles when things start to go wrong – that familiar tweak in the IT band, the pain in the butt associated with Piriformis syndrome, the list goes on. The question is, "Why do we get these problems?" Often it is our body's way of compensating for a misaligned pelvis.

The sacrum and the ilium form the sacroiliac joint. If this joint is stuck or misaligned, it will not be able to move in its normal pattern. This will create pull on the muscles that act around it. Some muscles will compensate by becoming overactive. For example the Piriformis will start to contract or be overworked trying to help the joint. This will be felt as a pain in the hip or butt. The Piriformis muscle is not alone in compensating for lack of movement of the sacroiliac joint. Any of the muscles that attach through the pelvis can be affected:

The hamstrings may become chronically tight
The adductors may get strained
The hip flexors may become chronically tight
The low back may become tight and sore.

The problems will also continue down the biomechanical chain: if the glute medius can't function properly because the pelvis is misaligned, it will not be able to stabilize the hip. When heel strike occurs, the knee will now rotate excessively because the hip is unstable – leading to medial knee pain.

If you ever notice that you stretch and stretch and stretch but can't seem to get a muscle to relax, chances are you have a misalignment. If the bones that the muscles attach to aren't in the proper position, there is no way the muscles can relax – they will be overactive. Once proper pelvic mechanics are restored (often through chiropractic adjustments), the muscles can relax and be stretched effectively. Injuries are minimized and function is maximized.

In the internal martial arts, internal strength is achieved through relaxation. If one part of the body is chronically tight and numb to feeling, then this creates an area through which connection is difficult to feel. To the extent that the pelvic floor is involved in stabilizing the pelvis, intra-abdominal pressure, and breathing, it makes logical sense to do more than pay attention to what's going on "down there."

In many internal martial art classes, the focus is typically on teaching forms, push-hands, drills, and sparring. Little time is spent with the instructor making repeated, ever more miniscule, externally subtle yet internally dramatic, postural adjustments to help identify and release ever more subtle levels of chronic tension. From my experience, until you begin working at this level, then you really are not on the road to developing internal skill sets no matter how firmly you believe you have "qi flowing".

You have probably heard the saying, "Use your Yi to lead your Qi". This is kind of easy to conceptually understand but is more often than not, functionally misunderstood.

The Essence of Taiji Qigong: The Internal Foundation of Taijiquan, Second Edition. (1998) Yang, Jwing-Ming.

Please pay attention to the word "lead." Qi behaves like water – it can be led, but it cannot be pushed. The more you intend to push Qi, the more you will tense, and the worse the Qi will circulate. Therefore, the trick is to always place your Yi ahead of your Qi. (pg 73)

I've heard the following analogy which fits well here. Imagine a stream three meters wide shore-to-shore and two meters of that width are blocked by rocks and other obstructions. This leaves only one meter for the water to move through. Only through the effort of removing the blockages can the water flow naturally. In this analogy, the body is the streambed, the blockages are fascial adhesions, scar tissue, chronic tension and the water is the "qi".

No amount of "Yi leading the Qi" will get that water to move *through* those rocks and other obstructions. Because of those blockages, water backs-up which causes different problems upstream. Even if you could feel your qi flowing through that one meter, if you can't feel the blockage, then you don't know that you have another two meters to work with, to develop that much more power!

A functional understanding of "the Yi leads the Qi" is to focus on removing blockages where you want qi flow which will then allow qi to naturally flow where it was previously blocked from flowing. Focus on identifying and releasing chronic holding patterns and discover the amazing results of this very mundane and ordinary effort.

I'd like to close this chapter with one more excerpt. This will become relevant in the following chapter: Comfort Level 4: Experiencing Your Pelvic-Emotional Connection.

The Body Reveals: What Your Body Says About You. (1984). By Ron Kurtz and Hector Prestera, M.D.

It should be clear by now that tension in one area reflects back onto many others. In a sense, even a single tension is never really isolated because it includes compensations. Perhaps the two most contained expressive movements in the body are those of the pelvis and the breath. (pg. 58)

These individuals may be viewed as being afraid to let go, since the high charge they are carrying may be sensed as explosive. This anxiety is often associated with the question, "What will happen if I let go?" When such an individual is asked to describe what might happen, the reply is often "I don't really know." The sense is one of an unknown force. (pg. 61)

11

Comfort Level 2: Locating Your Pelvis Externally

I don't like being called "Elvis the Pelvis". That's gotta be one of the most childish expressions I've ever heard coming from an adult. - Elvis Presley

Introduction

We need look no further than our pop-culture icons for some pretty explicit "hints" of where the pelvis is and how it can move. Elvis Presley's 1956 performance of the song, Hound Dog, many of the 1960s California beach movie dance scenes, Michael Jackson's "pelvis thrust", and Beyonce's "booty shake" or TV's currently popular Dancing with the Stars, provide several good examples. However, having the ability to move this way is no guarantee that the muscles we need to relax are in fact relaxed. On the other hand, the ability to move this way indicates a pelvis that is a bit more free and open than frozen.

This section provides both a few very rudimentary methods to help you locate your pelvis and pelvic floor from the outside as well as exercises I've excerpted from others' websites. Depending on your purpose and the degree to which you run into your social-cultural taboos regarding this area of the body, locating and palpating your body with the conscious intention to learn may be challenging. If you can do these in front of a mirror you can get both external visual feedback as well as an internal feeling kind of feedback.

Methods

1. Sit on a hard surface. Feel the bones that touch that hard surface. These bones are the bottoms of the two ilia, the two sides of the pelvis.

2. While standing, put your hands on the sides of your hips. Move one leg then the other. Feel the movement of your upper femur under your hand. Notice how high and to the side of the pelvis the leg attaches. The legs attach high and on the outside, not down in the crotch.

3. Stand with both legs straight. Notice how the pelvis is fairly level. Bend one leg and allow the bent-leg side of the pelvis to drop. Repeat on the other side. This can also be done while sitting.

4. Stand with both legs straight. Arch your back tipping your pelvis forward. Straighten your back driving your tailbone under and tipping the pelvis backward. Repeat. This can also be done while sitting. This is known as an anterior-posterior pelvic tilt.

5. **Ode to the Pelvic Floor.** Angela Barsotti. http://pilatesunion.com/news/34/

   If you want to meet it <your pelvic floor>, sit in a regular kitchen type chair with your feet flat on the floor. Imagine you have to pee like you never have in your life (or lift and hold your pelvic floor) and then take three deep breaths. Then, let go like you finally went to the bathroom and take three more breaths. See how you couldn't breathe when you were tight and locked but you could when you let go? Say hello to your pelvic floor.

6. **Finding and activating pelvis floor muscles.** (2011). Author known as Left Wing Taoist. http://internalkungfuireland.blogspot.com/2011/11/finding-and-activating-pelvis-floor.html

My favorite image for getting the pelvic floor muscles in on an exercise is to think of bringing the sit bones together and up. The sit bones are the bony parts that you feel under you when you sit up straight on a firm surface. This is what is erroneously described as squeezing your anus. Correct description is lifting your perineum. What you need to do is engage the pelvic floor muscles. This will lift your anus not squeeze it but the effect will be that your butt cheeks will be squeezed together effectively squeezing your anus. Your pelvis will also be rotated forward and upward. This will also lift and pull in your genitals. You know the iron balls trick, where one guy sits in a narrow horse stands, and someone kicks him between his legs with a lifting kick, with no effect. You do it by lifting the pelvic floor. This rotates and lifts the butt muscles, and moves your genitals out of the way.

7. **Pelvic Biomechanics.** (1997) SportsMed Web. http://www.rice.edu/~jenky/sports/pelvic.biomech.html

    ...understand that sometimes abnormal pelvic motion is merely a result of a problem elsewhere. Looking at, and correcting, abnormal pelvic motion can help you discover these hidden problems. Clues of pelvic imbalance:

    a) Look at the wear on your shoes, if it is asymmetric, then you know that one leg is doing something different. This may not involve the pelvis but it is a consideration.

8. Perform a one leg squat, first with one leg and then the other. Go down to about a 90-degree bend in the knee. Watch yourself in the mirror. If balance is harder, or you find that one side seems weaker, tight, painful, or less coordinated, then you need to look more closely at pelvic biomechanics.

9. **Qigong Massage: Fundamental Techniques for Health and Relaxation** (2005) by Yang Jwing-ming.

In Chinese medicine and Qigong, the Huiyin is considered one of the most important cavities. It is the junction of many vessels... Stimulating the Huiyin cavity will improve the exchange of Qi among the vessels... When you massage this gate, spread your partner's legs a comfortable distance apart. Press gently on the Huiyin cavity with your middle finger and circle around. If you use your right hand, circling clockwise will lead Qi upward to the brain, and counterclockwise will lead Qi downward to the legs... (pg. 270-271)

10. **The Pelvic Floor Paradox.** by Leon Chaitow, ND, DO. December 2006. Vol 6, Issue 12. http://www.massagetoday.com/mpacms/mt/article.php?id=13515

A yoga therapist had then advised her to purchase a tennis ball and sit on it with the ball (placed on a firm surface such as a carpeted floor) strategically placed under the perineum, between anus and the vagina; and to allow the pressure onto the ball to deeply relax the pelvic floor muscles for five to 10 minutes daily. She reported that this procedure was somewhat uncomfortable at first, but that the effects were dramatic in terms of her symptoms. I have since recommended this to several patients for home use and all have reported benefit.

Don't Forget the Psychological Aspect
It's essential to note that in many such cases of clenched pelvic floor muscles, there is a background of assault or abuse (although a great many seem to be caused by nothing more than mechanically-produced, excessive tone with a background of dance, athletics and bad Pilates). Where there is a psychosocial or psychosexual element to the condition, appropriate professional support usually is needed along with bodywork.

11. **Pelvic Floor Strengthening: Pelvic Floor Contraction and a Word of Caution about doing Pelvic Floor Exercise.**
    (August 23, 2009) by Anne Asher.
    http://backandneck.about.com/od/pelvicfloor/ss/pelvicfloorstre_2.htm

    Pelvic floor contraction is a squeeze of the muscles of the bottom of your seat in an inward and upward direction. This is the action we all perform when we are controlling our bowels and bladder, including stopping the flow of urine.

    It is not advisable to practice pelvic floor strengthening exercises while you are emptying your bladder. Therefore, do not use stopping the flow of urine as a strengthening exercise for the pelvic floor muscles. Use it only as a way of finding and assessing the muscles (as described in the next section).

    Chiarelli explains that the complexities of a functioning bladder go beyond the muscular control offered by the pelvic floor (or any) muscles. While the pelvic floor muscles are a decided influence on bladder control, they are not in charge of the entire workings of the bladder; therefore, stopping the flow of urine as a regular practice may alter the function of your bladder for the worse.

12. **Pelvic Floor Strengthening: Tips and Considerations.**
    (August 23, 2009) by Anne Asher.
    http://backandneck.about.com/od/pelvicfloor/ss/pelvicfloorstre_7.htm

    Many people, especially in the beginning of their program, will have some problems isolating the pelvic floor muscles from the other muscles of the hips and pelvis. This is understandable, as the outer hip muscles are large and powerful. A key to success is to learn to recognize the feeling of just the pelvic floor muscles contracting, without the buttock muscles. To remove the buttock muscles from the movement you can practice pelvic floor contractions while standing with your legs wide apart and your heels out wider than your toes (a toed-in position of the feet). Do not do this if it increases your back pain, however. Once you are confident that you can perform pelvic floor contractions without using your butt muscles, you can do them correctly in whatever position you wish.

As with any exercise program, starting your pelvic floor strengthening program too vigorously can be a potential source of injury, fatigue or frustration. Start from the strength level you possess now and build slowly but consistently. Keeping track of the number of reps and seconds held as you go will allow you to increment the level of challenge in a sane and results-oriented way over the long term.

The most well-known pelvic floor exercises are the Kegels. The exercise presented here is essentially a Kegel exercise.

What Happens in the Pelvis Doesn't Stay in the Pelvis. (Nov 3, 2012) by Al Bingham. http://transformationzoneyoga.com/2012/11/03/what-happens-in-the-pelvis-doesnt-stay-in-the-pelvis/

Don't Engage Your Pelvic Floor Unless You've Had a Really Long Courtship. In some cultures, it's cool for one person to tell another, "Engage So-and-So" even though no relationship has been cultivated. And hey, sometimes that works out. Just like artificially engaging your pelvic floor muscles works out sometimes. Perhaps a better strategy is to ask those muscles: what turns you on? You know what we'll hear: actions. So if you suspect someone's pelvic floor isn't turning on, don't yell at it (engage! activate! lift!), instead, learn what movement patterns turn those muscles on and then trace their movement patterns to see whether they're getting those motions (or not).

Male Pelvic Floor: Advanced Massage and Bodywork - Welcome by Jeff Gibson. http://www.malepelvicfloor.com/

All men can benefit from getting to know their pelvic floor, yet massage and bodywork rarely if ever includes these muscles. If you are curious to learn more and are open to exploring this area, massage and bodywork is an excellent and rewarding way to do so. You will learn where your pelvic floor is, what it feels like, what the muscles do, how they are related to the integrity of your core, and how they support the functions associated with them. You may also become aware of emotional and energetic aspects of this key area as well as excess tension or weakness, and how these affect other areas of your body.

What a Waist. (June 22, 2010) by Katy Bowman. http://www.alignedandwell.com/katysays/what-a-waist/

You Don't Know Squat. (June 2, 2010) by Katy Bowman.http://www.alignedandwell.com/katysays/you-dont-know-squat/

De Stress with Pelvic Floor Awareness Exercise Part 1 (May 30, 2012) with Michelle Alva. http://www.youtube.com/watch?v=_jWCCLG46js

Summary

While these are not the only exercises, nor may these be the most suitable exercises for you at this time, I think these exercises serve as examples of how you can begin to develop a feel for your pelvis and pelvic area. I had not tried many of these methods before I found them for this book.

Regarding the tennis ball exercise, under the suggestion of my Wujifa instructor, I tried this method early in my experimenting with relaxing my pelvic floor but found it too uncomfortable to continue. I know now that that discomfort was an indication of how tense my muscles were! More recently I was able to sit on a baseball pressing into my pelvic floor with only mild discomfort; an indication to me of the level of relaxation achieved over the years!

Regarding squats, when I began learning Tai-chi I was able to do one-legged squats. Unfortunately, I did not continue this practice. Many years later, while practicing two-legged squats, I assumed that both legs were equally bearing their fair share of weight. When I tried one-legged squats, I discovered that both legs were only equally bearing weight down to a point after which I was unconsciously shifting the weight to the left leg because the right leg had no strength. Years of physical therapy later, I can now do one-legged squats again, pretty equally with both legs. This is yet another example both of how the body naturally compensates and in turn, how invisible chronic tension can be to our awareness!

12

Rounding the Crotch

Chen Tai-chi Chuan stylists speak of the need for the crotch (dang) to be round (yuan) as a method to develop full-body connection and internal strength. While not all internal martial art styles talk about rounding the crotch, I consider rounding the crotch a description of a feature that is (or should be!) common to all internal martial arts; namely, internal connection. I believe that the Chinese cultural concept or quality of round is also a desired kinesthetic quality in the body. (See "Appendix C: American-Chinese Cross-Cultural Analysis of Round for a discussion of round.) I believe this understanding of round is one way to describe the desired biomechanics through the pelvis.

Chinese Qi-gong (气功;qìgōng) teachers admonish students to make their body round-soft (圆软;yuánruǎn). Qigong teachers refer to "opening" (开;kāi) the Huiyin point (会阴;huìyīn) which is in the perineum or pelvic floor area.

At a very rudimentary, physical level, in the internal martial arts, rounding and opening can be loosely translated as "relaxing with an intention to developing connection". Methods that can help you learn how to relax the muscles of your pelvic floor are so rarely mentioned that we may consider these methods to be either unknown, overlooked, or kept secret. Given the current social stigma associated with discussing these methods in mixed audiences such as those found in public martial arts classes, often it is best to simply not raise the topic. And yet, knowing this practical information and practicing these methods may open a new way for you to improve your internal martial arts practice.

Here is an exercise from Wujifa class that demonstrates a very beginning level experience of rounding the crotch.

While I was standing in zhan zhuang, two of my Wujifa school brothers each grabbed one of my thighs and physically twisted my upper leg (twisting my thighs medially, from outside to inside) to force both of the greater trochanters to rotate forward. At the same time, my elder brother, our instructor, was adjusting my pelvis and torso to help me maintain proper structure. Eventually, after struggling through my resistance, my many counter-adjustments, I felt my weight drop so heavily into my legs that I literally could not remain standing and I collapsed to the floor!

While this method gave me a quick demonstration of rounding the crotch and an experience of how weak my legs were, it is my experience that such a demonstration has no long-term effects. Only through the personal work of relaxing the chronic tension of the pelvic floor, lower abdomen, and lower back will the femur heads naturally rotate forward on their own. And as they do, the legs slowly and naturally build the strength needed to support the dropping weight. It's a process.

One of the focal points of Wujifa zhan zhuang practice is the emphasis on rolling the greater trochanters forward. (The greater trochanter is the name for the top of the femur or "thigh bone" that you can palpate.) I don't know of any other school that approaches rounding the crotch in this way. In fact, working with the pelvis and greater trochanters has been one of the major and ongoing adjustments and refinements to my structure over the years. This training experience and how it is explained and approached in Wujifa class has contributed to my experiential understanding of rounding the crotch.

Before proceeding, take a moment to identify and palpate the bones of your hip region; the pelvis and greater trochanters. While standing, find the top of your thigh bone (the greater trochanter area) which is about a hand's length below the top of your pelvis on each side of your body. The top of the thigh bone that you feel is called the greater trochanter.

In many people, the greater trochanters are pulled slightly backward. This is typically due to chronic muscular tension throughout the pelvis, abdomen, and lower back. This creates a rather backward-orientation of your base of support (your legs), a narrowing of the distance between the

Rounding the Crotch

greater trochanters which results in a narrowing in the groin and a "holding up" of the weight of the torso. Chen Taijiquan stylists refer to this as an "A" or "V" shaped or "pointed" crotch.

You may also notice that your feet "naturally" point outward when you stand without thinking about the position of your feet. Assuming a normal healthy body and disregarding particular physiological or clinical conditions, it is possible that the tension in the lower back which torques the femurs slightly backward also transmits that same twist to the feet. And so in this way, the "natural" position of the feet can be an indicator of tight muscles in the lower back.

For example, a tight gluteus maximus muscle is an obvious target because the deepest quarter of the muscle connects the rear of the sacrum to the top of the femur (thigh) and three quarters connect to the top of the tibia (lower leg) through a length of ligament known as the iliotibial tract (or I.T. Band). Contracting the gluteus maximus muscles laterally rotates the thigh at the hip (from a knee forward to a knee outward position) and contracting it also extends or raises the knee at the hip.

What I've learned through long practice is that relaxing the muscles of the pelvic floor, the abdomen, and lower back allows the greater trochanters to rotate slightly forward. This creates a more sideward-orientation of your base of support (your legs), a widening of the distance between the greater trochanters which results in a widening in the groin and a "dropping" of the weight of the torso. This is referred to as an arched or "n" or round shaped crotch.

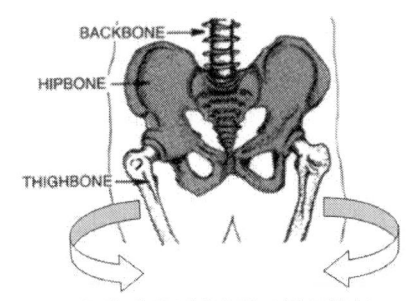

Rounding the Crotch for Tai chi and Zhan Zhuang.
Relax pelvic floor and lower back to allow the femur heads to rotate forward.

Secrets of the Pelvis for Martial Arts

Rotating the femurs to allow the greater trochanters to move forward seems like a subtle movement however, the result is a huge change to the angle of the force vectors of the weight of the torso through the pelvis into the femurs. At this time, I am able to roll both my greater trochanters forward by about one inch (2-3 cm) and I notice a big difference in my ability to "drop into my legs". I still have much more work to do.

For a nice article on working the musculature of the pelvis, please see *Basic Tips for Zhan Zhuang and the Pelvis* by Richard Taracks http://wujifaliangong.blogspot.com/2009/06/basic-tips-for-zhan-zhang-and-pelvis.html Here is an excerpt:

> When one simply relaxes more deeply or as one learns to relax the muscles of the lower back and supporting muscles and relax the glutes while practicing stance training then the back can lengthen and the femoral heads of the right and left legs can be allowed to widen. This gives more room for the pelvis to adjust on the hip joints and with the opening/lengthening of the spine "allows" the tailbone or sacrum to shift and drop downward in these practices. This is VERY different than tucking.

To the untrained eye, there is no outward visible difference between my standing with my femoral heads pulled back or more relaxed at the side. However to someone who has achieved a greater level of relaxation, my chronic holding patterns are obvious. Hence, the written descriptions distinguishing an "A" or "V" or "sharp" shaped crotch from an "arch" or round shaped crotch.

What I understand now is that the Chen Taiji saying of *round the crotch* (as opposed to the misinterpretation of "relax the crotch") may be related to two widely different yet completely related elements: a broader Chinese cultural understanding of *round* and the mechanical stability of the stone arch bridge.

In Chinese culture, the word for round (yuan), as you might expect, expresses characteristics of shape. However, the deeper and broader cultural symbolism and meaning of round expresses a quality of connectedness, of completeness, of wholeness, of integration. My understanding is that achieving roundness in the crotch connects the legs to the torso through the pelvis in a way which we are not normally accustomed. (Again, see "Appendix C: American-Chinese Cross-Cultural Analysis of Round" for a cross-cultural analysis of round.)

When considering a stone arch bridge as a model or analogy for the functioning of the pelvis and legs, the feet and legs form each side of the base of the arch bridge and the perineum is the "key stone" at the top between the two bases. When the greater trochanters are more side-ward oriented rather than backward oriented, then the legs and perineum more imitate the structural stability of an arch bridge.

Arch bridge Yunlong Lake, Xuzhou, China. by Peter Griffin
http://www.publicdomainpictures.net/view-image.php?image=27190&picture=arch-bridge

And so, my conclusion regarding *rounding the crotch* is that:

- A *rounded* crotch or perineum or pelvic floor is one that is relaxed, not limp or weak, not rigid, yet full and alive and contributes to the harmony, fluidity, continuity, connectedness, and structural completeness of the whole body.

- It is a mistake to try to mechanically create the shape of a *rounded crotch*. Simply spreading your feet further apart does not create the *quality* of *roundness*.

- While the shape may appear as being more *round*, it is not *round* unless there is a *quality* of *roundness*. Relaxing, grounding, and connecting the torso to the legs through the pelvis create *roundness*.

- Relaxing the muscles of the pelvic floor and the lower back happens with intention. An initial intention or purpose might be to intentionally work on identifying and relaxing tension in the abdomen, pelvic floor and lower back.

Relaxing and developing the quality of round by incorporating and integrating the abdomen, lower back and pelvic floor contributes to a strong and stable zhan zhuang stance and stepping.

13

Comfort Level 3: Working with Your Pelvis Internally

With correct practice, the invisible becomes subtle.
With more practice, the subtle becomes obvious.

Introduction

Shhh! Guess what? I've got a secret. Promise not to tell? OK. Here it is. "THE BIG SECRET"! How big is it? It's so big that I had to write an entire book just to ease you into this one chapter! Are you ready? This is the chapter that talks about what martial artists don't openly talk about. And yet, medical and various therapeutic practitioners speak openly as you can see in the Appendices. Yes, this is the part of training that is so often avoided or overlooked.

This is the chapter where you might shift from feeling comfortable to feeling uncomfortable. I know that I sure did when I first heard about this level of working with my own body! Whatever reaction you have is perfectly normal for you. Notice it. Acknowledge it. As we say in Wujifa, "You are where you are and that's where you start."

Here are methods that I have either used myself or have read about. As with any practice, first verify with your physician that it is appropriate and safe for you according to your physical situation. You are responsible for your own practice!

Remember that the goal of these exercises is to identify and release tensions and holding patterns. Through the practice of relaxing, we develop the body to get it to the place where we can begin to do the work of feeling whole-body connectedness. Everyone's body is different. Maybe none of these methods or tools is needed to help you discover that connected feeling. Maybe some of these will be helpful. I just don't know. It's hard to say.

Remember how item #22 in the above list, "Twenty-Three Things to Know about Your Pelvis" mentioned how the pelvic floor is innervated? If you've forgotten this already, here it is again:

> The muscles and organs of the pelvic floor are innervated by the pudendal nerve which emerges from S2-S4 on both sides of the sacrum and branches into three sections; one branch goes to the anal-rectal area, another goes to the perineum, and another goes to the genitals.

This becomes especially relevant now. The very nerves that are associated with genital stimulation and pleasure are but one branch of three. Another branch innervates the perineum (the area between the genitals and anus) and another branch innervates the anal-rectal area. The point is that when working on relaxing the pelvic floor using the methods described below, feelings of genital stimulation and/or pleasure may result. When you know that these feelings are quite natural due to the way this area is innervated, then any emotional reactions that you may become aware of may be addressed from this understanding.

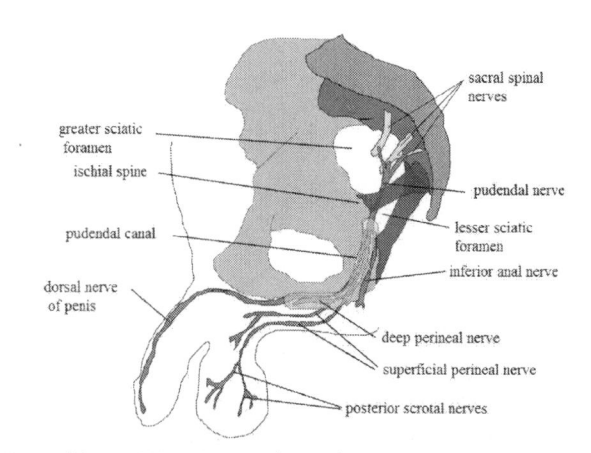

http://en.wikipedia.org/wiki/File:Pudendal_nerve.svg

Methods

Before we get into specific methods, let's look at chapter 4.4, "Treatment of Sexual and Pelvic Floor Dysfunctions" of the book, *The Pelvic Floor* by Beate Carriere and Cynthia Markel Feldt (2006) where she says:

> When the patient is able to relax and breathe toward the pelvic floor, she should try to relax the gluteus muscles, hamstrings and adductors. Because these muscles almost always contract along with the pelvic floor muscles, they have to be relaxed consciously before further relaxation of the pelvic floor can be attempted.
>
> It is best to start routinely with the relaxation of the anus, since clinical experience shows that this is the part of the pelvic floor the patient feels most distinctly. However, if the symptoms focus on the anus, it is best to start with the anterior part. (pg. 408).

Let's focus for a moment. What did she just say? "It is best to start routinely with the relaxation of *the anus*, (emphasis added) since clinical experience shows that this is the part of the pelvic floor the patient feels most distinctly." Assuming there are no clinical symptoms, start with the relaxation of the anus.

When I began working at this level, I used a couple of the methods described below. The experience, insights and lessons learned about my own body are at a level which are both deeply personal and difficult to put into words. If and when you begin working at this level, you too may find your experiences, insights, and lessons learned to be not only somehow unexplainable but also very personal. In my experience, we may share general holding patterns which can be traced to culture, values, upbringing, etc.., however, the particularities of your experience will be very different from mine and for this reason, I do not believe that you would necessarily benefit from reading about my experiences even if I could put them into words. And so at this point, I will defer to providing previously published methodologies, a few of which I encountered when I first began working at this level.

Secrets of the Pelvis for Martial Arts

Let me offer one tip. Monitor your emotional reaction as you read through these six methods. Your initial reaction or even a lack of reaction to simply reading these methods should be a good first insight about where you are at this point in time. Keep in mind that the immediate goal of these exercises is to identify and release tensions and holding patterns for the larger goal of developing the ability to feel into this area and to develop a feeling of connectedness between the legs and torso through the pelvis.

1. **Internal Perineal Massage via the Vagina**. The Journal of Midwifery and Women's Health. Vol 50, No1, January/February 2005 (pg. 63-64)
http://www.midwife.org/ACNM/files/ccLibraryFiles/Filename/000000000656/Perineal%20Massage%20in%20Pregnancy.pdf

   <Note: While the focus of this article is on preventing tearing during childbirth, I've included it here since it is a method of massaging the perineum.>

2. **Anal Peripheral Prostrate Massage**. William Zmachinsky
http://www.prostate-massage-and-health.com/Anal-peripheral-prostate-massage.html
   You are actually going to be massaging inside of your anus here. So, please check with your doctor to make sure you have no medical condition that would make this unadvisable for you or put you at risk of injury.

   First: Lie down on your back. Lubricate your middle finger with some KY Jelly. (That is what your Urologist uses during your exam).

   Insert your lubricated finger about 1 - 1 1/2 inches into your anus. Make sure your finger nail is cut short and filed smooth, so that you don't cut or scratch your rectum.

Comfort Level 3: Working with Your Pelvis Internally

When you insert your finger, you will feel how tight and sensitive this muscle is. It feels like a small tight rubber tire around your finger. The more sensitive it feels, the more it needs massage.

After performing the Anal Peripheral Prostate Massage, you may feel a little exhausted. This is a natural reaction anytime you release a large amount of tension in your body.

3. **A Too Tight Pelvic Floor.** (April 25, 2012). Katy Bowman
http://www.alignedandwell.com/katysays/atootightpelvicfloor/

Because these muscles have been held in tension it can be difficult to know how to relax. I have found it very helpful to use a finger inserted at the vaginal opening to assist with the cue to "drop" the pelvic muscle downward/backward. A slight pressure onto the muscle provides stimulus to tell the muscle to let go. This can be helpful for the first few visits until the person has confidence in performing the relaxation on their own.

4. **Find the Inward Squeeze.** (August 23, 2009). Anne Asher
http://backandneck.about.com/od/pelvicfloor/ss/pelvicfloorstre_3.htm

Stopping the flow of urine is a good technique for finding out how the pelvic floor muscles feel when they are in action. This is the first step in creating a maintaining a strengthening program for them. If you are able to stop the flow of urine completely and instantly, you are ready to embark on the exercise program. If not, the finger test described below will help you to recognize and assess your own pelvic floor contractions.

For Women
Insert 2 fingers into your vagina and contract.

For Men

Insert one finger into the rectum and tighten your muscles around it.

When you find your inner squeeze, it will feel like the opposite of bearing down to make a bowel movement. It is a drawing in and up around your inserted fingers. You can aim to bring your tailbone and your pubic bone together, and while you may not notice this actually happening, using the image might get your pelvic floor muscles into a working contraction.

While you are doing this test, continue breathing -- holding your breath alters the way in which muscles are being used, and defeats the purpose of the test.

Take heart, the contraction you feel may be small, but once you locate a contraction you are ready to strengthen your pelvic floor muscles with exercise.

5. **Determine Strength and Endurance of Your Pelvic Floor Contractions.** (August 23, 2009). Anne Asher http://backandneck.about.com/od/pelvicfloor/ss/pelvicfloorstre_4.htm

This step is an assessment of the strength and endurance capacity of the pelvic floor muscles:

First, test yourself for the length of time you can hold a pelvic floor contraction. To do this, repeat the finger test, but this time count the number of seconds you can hold the muscles up in the inward squeeze. This is a measure of muscular endurance, or how long can your pelvic floor muscles can go before they begin to tire.

After you know the length of time your pelvic floor muscles can endure, the next test is for the strength of the contraction. In other words, how many of these contractions can you perform before the muscle becomes fatigued? Perform as many of them as you can. Count as you go and take note of the number.

The third step is to clock how much rest you need between your contractions.

The final step in the strength and endurance assessment is to test for the performance of fast working muscle fibers of the pelvic floor muscles. To do this perform inward upward squeezes just as fast and as hard as you can, and count the number you can do before fatiguing. Do not stop for a break until you are done with the whole set.

Make note of all these measurements so that you can see how you progress with the strengthening program.

Chiarelli recommends seeing a urinary continence specialist if you have not been able to locate the contraction of your pelvic floor muscles at any time during this assessment.

6. **What is a Rectal Dilator?** wiseGEEK: Clear Answers for Common Questions
http://www.wisegeek.com/what-is-a-rectal-dilator.htm

A rectal dilator is a manual medical tool designed to help train the anus to relax to a greater degree. People use the instrument to treat issues such as constipation and hemorrhoids, as well as to reduce pain during anal intercourse. Although a person can purchase a set of dilators discretely online, obtaining and using a set with medical supervision is ideal. The devices have been in use at least since the turn of the 20th century, with early doctors making benefits claims well beyond what the dilators actually do. Modern doctors and manufacturers are more careful with their advertising and have proven the effectiveness of dilators for anal stretching through scientific research.

The degree to which a person needs to relax the anus varies. Additionally, it can be painful to use an instrument that is overly large at the first point in treatment. Subsequently, manufacturers produce rectal dilators in sets, with each set having three to six tools. The user starts with the smallest size, moving through the larger instruments as he becomes comfortable.

Regardless of which reason a person needs a rectal dilator, cultural influences can cause people to feel somewhat embarrassed about using one — depending on their background, a person may regard inserting anything into the anus as taboo or "dirty." Physicians view a rectal dilator as a medical instrument and see the pain relief available, however, even if it is used to aid sex acts. Individuals who need one <of> these tools thus should not be afraid to seek physician assistance in obtaining a set. In fact, using the dilators under medical supervision is ideal, as the physician can monitor the patient's relaxation progress and underlying conditions.

Summary

If you've read this far, you've probably realized by now that the approach outlined in this book is completely different from the typical, "Imagine your Qi flowing" approach. We're not in Kansas anymore, Dorothy! There are many paths up the mountain! This is one path and it is a particularly functional path.

The following information may be common sense to many but here are some things to consider if you choose to explore the above mentioned methods on your own:

- Although the pelvic floor muscles may be chronically tense, the internal organs are soft and susceptible to damage. Do your reading. Understand what you are doing. Proceed at your own risk.

Comfort Level 3: Working with Your Pelvis Internally

- Sanitation is the number one priority. Depending on the method, latex gloves or a similar protective covering for your hand or individual finger should be used. Ensure you clean up thoroughly and properly.

- It is best to "relieve yourself" first. This will both reduce the muscular tension of holding and the need to jump on the toilet as you progressively relax during a session.

You may find that relaxing during a session results in even more "movement" of which you were previously unaware. Therefore, it is best to practice these methods in the bathroom or W.C. where a toilet and sink are readily available.

You will naturally experiment with and find the body position and materials that are easiest for you to work with in the most relaxed way. The purpose is to relax. Remember, for internal martial arts we engage these methods to help relax the crotch, hips and waist to help us develop the "round crotch" quality.

Remember, relaxing the muscles of the pelvis and pelvic floor is a process and not a one-time event. It will likely take many sessions over weeks or months or longer to notice and feel a new level of relax show up in your internal martial arts practice. Follow-up "maintenance" massage sessions are helpful.

Above all, use common sense. These methods are not to be practiced as a contest or competition. Think of this more as "self-care". Be gentle with yourself. Aim for slow, incremental progress over the long term. Think "process" instead of "goal". If you start down this road, know that you are embarking on a journey. Addressing the tension in the pelvic floor, the crotch, is one of many areas to address on the path of relaxing and developing whole-body connection.

The rectal or anal dilator is also commonly known as a "butt plug". (See Appendix D: Historical Use of Medical Rectal Dilators.) You may find this product under either of these names. Due to the size range of these devices, it is best to start with the smallest size. If you force yourself in using one that is larger than your muscle is able to relax and stretch, it is possible to dilate or stretch the anal sphincter muscle too far which can actually result in clinical symptoms requiring medical attention. If you try this method without medical supervision, you must be able to distinguish a safe stretch from the creation of a clinical symptom. Even if you think you did not over-extend the stretch, you may find you have already unintentionally hurt yourself. Everyone's body is different. What is safe for one person may be damaging for another.

A common fear or misperception is that relaxing the muscles around the anal sphincter will cause loss of control of the bowels. I have not had this experience. Regardless of the level of tension or relaxation, the anal sphincter seems to remain closed naturally. In my experience, this fear was just one of the many reasons (excuses) to not explore and relax this part of my own body. Using a dilator helps the surrounding muscles reach a new level of reduced stricture around the diameter of the dilator. When the dilator is removed, the muscles are tense to the diameter of the dilator, meaning they are more relaxed after the dilator is removed. As I said in the introduction to this section every body is different. Just because I had one experience does not guarantee that you will have a similar experience. Do your own research. Proceed according to your particular situation.

As noted in "The Tennis Ball Trick", bear in mind that one possible side-effect of releasing tension bound in particular muscles is the concurrent release of bio-chemicals or emotions that may be bound up in the tension. In an area of the body such as the pelvic floor which may also carry an emotional-charge, even if the "charge" is taboo, releasing this bound-up tension may result in some kind of emotional release or shift. I've seen huge personality changes in school brothers over the years. Relaxing and letting go is powerful stuff!

14

Brief Introduction to Mind-Body, Psycho-Somatics

In high school biology class I developed a dis-integrated, system-isolated view of my body as being an upright skeleton upon which were added muscles, blood vessels, nerves, and organs all wrapped in skin. I viewed my body as a collection of parts; the body as a finely tuned machine.

During college and my early Tai-chi years, my view of who I am changed to a confused amalgam consisting of:

- A New Age holistic triangle: Body (Physical), Mind (Emotional / Psychological) and Spirit

- The body as energy: Indian Yogic Chakras or Chinese Qi circulating in Meridians

Even though these perspectives helped me to explore a conceptual shift in the direction of integrating my disassociated habit of being, neither of these concepts contributed to my developing a kinesthetic feeling sensibility of my own corporeal reality of life in and under my own skin. A functional re-integration wouldn't begin to occur for me until many years later when I began receiving Rolfing massage and practicing Wujifa zhan zhuang.

The Great Stillness: The Water Method of Taoist Meditation
Series, Vol. 2 (2001). Bruce Frantzis.

The Way of Liu: Reconnecting with Your Internal Environment
We are all born with the natural ability to directly experience internal sensations, but in almost all of us it is lost before puberty. Why? Pick your theory: Is this a defense to avoid experiencing the mental and emotional horror of a previously experienced emotional trauma? Is it industrial society's inclination to reduce human beings to unfeeling machines? Is it a result of the emerging electronic world of image without substance, where sights and sounds are disembodied from human feeling? Or is it where "virtual reality" becomes the culture's new way of relating to the world with "virtual feeling, virtual sex, and virtual relationships"? Should we be in such a rush to jettison our humanity? (pg. 30)

For a historical context, my understanding is that the Western psycho-somatic "movement" originated with Wilhelm Reich (1897–1957) who was a student of Sigmund Freud (1856-1939) and by extension, a "classmate" of Carl Jung (1875-1961). Where Jung followed the mind only path of Freud, Reich followed the mind-body connection and developed methods to work on the mind through the body. Two of Reich's students, Alexander Lowen (1910-2008) and Ida Rolf (1896-1979) respectively established Bioenergetic Analysis and Structural Integration which later became known as Rolfing.

Other contemporaries of Wilhelm Reich, Ida Rolf, and Alexander Lowen include Frederick Matthias Alexander (1869 - 1955) developer of the Alexander Technique, and Moshé Feldenkrais (1904–1984) who developed the Feldenkrais Method. From what I've read, both these men developed their respective systems independently; not directly in the Freudian lineage. From these pioneers arose many other disciplines that work on the body-mind integration to varying degrees and levels.

Here are some excerpted paragraphs which succinctly explain Reich's contribution.

Brief Introduction to Mind-Body Psycho-Somatics

Wilhelm Reich and His Influence. (October 5, 2008). Victor Daniel
http://www.sonoma.edu/users/d/daniels/reichlecture.html

"Body Language" -- the term is now commonplace. It wasn't always that way. With Freud and psychoanalysis everything was the mind. Reich was the first to bring the body into psychoanalysis, and to physically touch the client.

THE BODY'S OUTWARD APPEARANCE IS AN ACCURATE REFLECTION OF WHAT'S HAPPENING INSIDE, said Reich. There is a basic mistake in idea, "I think,...I am." You can't change your thoughts at a basic level without change in your body, in what you do.

- Reich wanted a full-body emotional response to life. If you cover yourself up, may deaden pain, but also rob yourself of full joy.
- When someone inhibits an impulse they feel tension. Inhibited libido is tense muscles, sexual charm is relaxed muscles.

FUNCTIONS OF MUSCULAR ARMOR:
An armored person does not feel their armor as such. Reich believed that mind-body work is necessary for people to rid themselves of this armor.

BODY ARMOR AND CHARACTER ARMOR are essentially the same. Their function is trying to protect yourself against the pain of not expressing things that society says you may not express. Muscular armor is character armor expressed in body, muscular rigidity.

Armoring is the sum total of the muscular attitudes which a person develops as a defense against the breakthrough of emotions, especially anxiety, rage, sexual excitation. Character armor is the sum total of all the years of the muscular attitude that have also been incorporated in the person's character.

If you're not familiar with the writings of Wilhelm Reich or Alexander Lowen or the work of Bio-Energetic therapists, it might be difficult to grasp the full significance and everyday manifestation of the above summary. One less abstract way to understand and clinically see one result of emotional and character armor is to look at fascial adhesions. These arise in the body from repetitive motion, physical habits and/or physical injury. If you didn't watch "The Fuzz Speech" before, watch it now. I haven't found a more clear explanation and vivid demonstration of how our bodies get stuck.

Fascia and stretching: The Fuzz Speech. (Feb 7, 2009). Gil Hedley, Ph.D. http://www.youtube.com/watch?v=_FtSP-tkSug

And so if I change my language from the dualistic, disassociated, possessive "my body" to something my integrated like "me-body", this is a more concise understanding of the "I" that shows up at class and at practice. Some body parts move freely. Some muscles are rigid. Some muscle bands are stuck to others. I'm easy-going about some aspects of life. I hold rigidly to other aspects. Some aspects I can see. Other aspects I'm completely blind seeing to even after being pointed out to me. Some body-work feels great. Some body-work hurts. Sometimes the pain *is not* emotionally charged – there is only the physical pain of releasing a knotted muscle or fascial adhesion. Sometimes the pain *is* emotionally charged – the physical pain is not as great as the fear or sadness that manifests. Sometimes memories come rushing back and disappear as quickly. Whatever comes up is the "me-body". It's all me. Going through this process of relaxing and letting go and dealing with whatever comes up in the process is my internal gong-fu. It is the process of becoming a "black belt". It is the process of getting to a place where I can begin training in earnest.

If this got a bit abstract, let's look at an example from a popular movie, The Empire Strikes Back; the second of the 1980's Star Wars trilogy. There is one scene where Luke goes to Dagobah to receive Jedi training from Yoda. The following conversation takes place outside the dark cave:

Yoda: That place… is strong with the dark side of the Force.
A domain of evil it is. In you must go.
Luke: What's in there?
Yoda: Only what you take with you.
Yoda: Your weapons, you will not need them.

But Luke strapped on his weapons belt anyway. He did not know that what he was to face could not be defeated with weapons. The cave showed Luke his fear in the form of an illusion; his own belief, his own mental construct. He tried to kill what he was afraid of and discovered his own face; he is the creator of his own fears. Luckily, I don't have to fly to Dagobah to be trained by Yoda. I can find my own personally tailored Star Wars Jedi training "cave" in my own pelvis!

My understanding of the theory of Bioenergetic Analysis is that it looks at how emotions are stored in the body and through body work and talking, strives to open the body to get a vibration to move unimpeded through the body. Therefore, the therapy involves looking for and resolving the emotional-muscular holding patterns that block that vibration.

Even though Ida Rolf learned from Wilhelm Reich, my experience is that contemporary Rolfing massage therapists tend to limit their work to only the physical structure and do not counsel psychological issues. If psychological stuff comes up that needs discussing, then seeing a qualified counselor or psychotherapist can be very helpful in talking through the issue. Remember, for internal martial arts, the training directive is to relax and let go. Relaxing and letting go while maintaining structural integrity applies to all of who I am. To achieve the highest levels demands doing the deepest work. In the interest of full disclosure, yes, I have been to talk-therapists to talk-through stuff that came out during intense body-work sessions. It's all part of the process.

Here are a few more excerpts from various authors that describe the body-mind connection, specifically, the pelvis-mind or pelvis-emotion connection.

Anal Pleasure and Health: A Guide for Men and Women by Jack Morin, Ph.D. (1998) Chapter 6 "Mind and Body", (pg. 57-58)

Body and mind, anus and emotions, are in constant interrelationship... Animals and human infants exhibit this spontaneous defecation reaction to severe threat, but we soon learn that this response is inappropriate. Therefore, when adults are under high stress our natural response is to rigidify our anuses in an effort to counteract the urge to defecate. This is why most of us associate a tense anus with fear.

In civilized society many of our stress reactions are to internal threats. These are specific fears... or general anxieties.

The Distress Response in Aikido, Trauma Recovery, and Peacemaking. (2008). Paul Linden, Ph.D. http://www.being-in-movement.com/distress-response-aikido-trauma-recovery-and-peacemaking.htm

The body responds to any form of stress by contracting. When people feel threatened or challenged in any way, they typically contract their breathing, posture, movement, and attention, and this can take six related forms. It may take the form of tensing and bracing as a preparation for strength and effort. It may take the similar form of tensing and hardening in anger. It may show up as stiffening and constricting in fear. It may take the form of collapsing and becoming limp in defeat and resignation. It may manifest in numbing of specific areas of the body or in an overall state of dissociation. Or elements of these can combine.

The Pelvic Girdle: An approach to the examination and treatment of the lumbopelvic-hip region. 3rd edition. (2004). Diane Lee.

Altered afferent input from the articular mechanoreceptors can have profound influences on both static and dynamic pelvic girdle function. Several studies… have shown that changes in muscle fiber type, muscle bulk, and recruitment patterns occur with pain and pathology. However, simply relieving pain does not necessarily restore optimum function; these changes can remain even when pain subsides…. Changes in the proprioceptive and motor control systems alter movement patterns and strategies of load transfer. The result is less efficient movement, suboptimal function, a higher risk for recurrence of pain and injury…, and altered joint forces (due to altered axes of joint rotation) that may lead to earlier degenerative changes and pain. (pg. 37)

Consequently, the ability to transfer load through the pelvis effectively is dynamic and depends on:

- Optimal function of the bones, joints, and ligaments (form closure or joint congruency)
- Optimal function of the muscles and fascia (force closure)
- Appropriate neural function (motor control, emotional state) (pg. 42-43)

Emotional states (fight, flight, or freeze reactions) are physically expressed through muscle action and, when sustained, influence basic muscle tone and patterning… If the muscles of the pelvis become hypertonic, this state will increase compression of the SIJs… It is important to understand the patient's emotional state since the detrimental motor pattern can often only be changed by affecting the emotional state… Teaching individuals to be "mindful" or aware of what is happening in their body during times of physical and/or emotional loading can reduce sustained, unnecessary muscle tone and therefore joint compression... (pg. 54)

15

Comfort Level 4: Experiencing Your Pelvic-Emotional Connection

There are no secrets. There's only stuff you don't know.

Introduction

Here's what I have learned about the genital-emotional connection. The pelvic floor obviously includes the genitals though in our typical state of disassociation, the genitals are somehow considered existing by themselves "down there" somehow separate from the musculature and furthermore, somehow separate from emotions, personality and character. In this section, I will try to expose this disassociation and offer methods to re-establish connection.

Based on my experience, I have discovered in myself and have seen in others that working on the pelvis will bring up emotions related to sexual expression or repression. But expression and repression are rather broad brush-strokes. More specifically, emotions of fear initiated by any of a variety of life experiences can create patterns of tension and holding in the musculature of the pelvis which in turn inhibit or block the free-flow of one's sexual energy. Energetic blockages in the pelvis inhibit the ability to connect the legs to the torso. Thus to work on achieving whole-body connection and "qi flowing", it is necessary to discover, relax, and let go of these holding patterns. This, however, is easier said than done. But without working through this process, then a clean, whole-body-connectedness, a.k.a., internal strength, is not achievable. Holding creates blockages and these blockages are easily observable in others by those who have done the difficult work of releasing these blockages in themselves.

A typical blockage to working with the genital-emotional connection in the pelvis is a complete denial that such a connection exists and that this connection has anything to do with internal martial arts! In fact, this denial is a manifestation of a very powerful fear.

In my early Tai-chi years, I thought I could jump right into Taoist alchemy; working with the "subtle energies". In the end, whatever Taoist practices I toyed with yielded no demonstrable results. In hindsight, the reasons for this are many and now obvious. For example, I had not done the preliminary body-work to resolve fascial adhesions and let go of chronically tense muscles. I wasn't even aware of my own emotional-muscular holding patterns. I couldn't even feel into my body at a rudimentary level. And regarding my pelvis? What's that? Just how was I going to feel "subtle energies" when I couldn't even feel gross muscle tension? If I had to guess, I think a lot of people get stuck like I did and are completely blind to how they're stuck just like I was. I hope this book at least opens your eyes to areas in your training where you may currently have blind spots or problems.

Again, in the interest of full disclosure, I have never been a patient of a Bioenergetic therapist in a professional setting. I have however been fortunate to have worked with people skilled in Bioenergetics who have voluntarily shared their expertise in working with me in private over the years. Despite all the work I've done, and all the progress I've made, underneath it all, I'm still pretty stuck. It's like peeling the onion. Just when I get one area free and moving, then I discover a deeper area that is stuck or an emotional level where I'm stuck. I guess the beauty of all this work over time (gong-fu) is that I'm more accepting of the process and I'm not so stuck on achieving a limited goal. I know what I have to do to get unstuck and I'm afraid to do that. Fear is a powerful training partner on many levels!

If you're wondering, "Why don't you go see a Bioenergetic therapist in a professional setting? Wouldn't that help you make progress quicker?" The simple answer is that I'm afraid. And this too is one area where I'm stuck; where there is a blockage to actually bringing up and letting go of stuff I've become aware of but continue to deny addressing.

So, yes, if you allow yourself to work at this level you may discover some very personal emotional issues relating to your expression or repression of your sexuality. If you are interested in learning more, you may want to read books by Alexander Lowen which go into greater detail about these relationships.

The Body in Psychotherapy. (Sept 2000). Edward W. L. Smith

Lowen (1980) believes that sexuality is the "key to being," and that the pelvis is the keystone bone in the body arch. If the pelvic muscles are armored, then the pelvis has reduced motility, thus upsetting the balance and harmony of the entire body. (pg. 160)

Emotional and Physical Pain Activate Similar Brain Regions.
(2012, April 19). Fogel, A.
http://www.psychologytoday.com/blog/body-sense/201204/emotional-and-physical-pain-activate-similar-brain-regions

over the course of evolution, our bodies decided to take the economy route and use a single neural system to detect and feel pain, regardless of whether it is emotional or physical.

Here's the part that most psychologizing tends to leave out: the brain is massively interconnected with the rest of the body. ... In this way, every cell in the body – every cell -- is linked into the nervous system and as such, can be sensed and felt, whether or not we allow ourselves to be aware of this psychobiological fact…

In what way might emotions be embodied? All emotions have a motor component. Even if we try to hide our feelings, there will be micro-momentary muscular activation. The anterior cingulate is located right next to the premotor area, which begins the process of forming an emotional expression in the body. The premotor area connects to the motor cortex above it, and then back to the specific muscles of expression.

Emotional pain may be located in the body in those places where an expression was meant to happen but failed to materialize.

A Headache in the Pelvis: A New Understanding and Treatment for Chronic Pelvic Pain Syndromes. 6th edition. (2011). Wise, D. & Anderson, R. Occidental, CA: National Center for Pelvic Pain Research.

Basically, most people want the areas of the genital and rectum to work, but don't want to know much about them or to have to pay any attention to them.

These areas of the body are not treated with much respect. This is a truth that is reflected in how we word profanities. What do we call people at whom we are angry? Usually terms related to defecation or procreation are used in a derogatory way. Indeed, these are terms of denigration. In our culture, the genitals and rectum are shrouded in shame and guilt. As we discuss later, the genitals and rectum are areas that are often psychologically and energetically disowned by people. Being rejected in some way, it is not uncommon for people to try to distance themselves from these body parts by tightening against them. The healing of the abused pelvis, as Steven Levine has stated eloquently, in part involves bringing the genitals and rectum "back into the heart." This means changing one's attitude from shame, guilt, and rejection to compassion and appreciation.

Comfort Level 4: Experiencing Your Pelvic-Emotional Connection

Methods

1. **The Deep Six, Part 1**. (Originally published in Massage & Bodywork magazine, June/July 2003). Thomas Myers
http://www.massagetherapy.com/articles/index.php/article_id/412/The-Deep-Six-Part-1

   First off, all of the "deep six" are part of a larger series of muscles centered around the greater trochanter.

   These muscles mostly go from the back of the trochanter to the back of the pelvis,...

   These muscles are often overused by those who need to "control," and this tightness is often accompanied by tightness in the pelvic floor and anus as well.

   There's a story in the bodywork world that goes: A baby doesn't get voluntary control of the anal sphincter until around 2 years old, so if a mother is trying to toilet-train a child before then, the only way the poor kid can please Mom is to use these deep butt muscles as an alternative to close off the sphincter -- and therefore the tightness in these muscles gets associated with not making a mess, pleasing Mom, and, of course, being "in control." Whether this story is technically accurate, there is certainly a commonality between the two meanings of "up tight," and it is worth considering that chronic tension in this area has a psychological basis.

   The other common psychological consideration here is that when the coccyx is pushed forward, the tail is literally tucked between the legs. This is a common posture of submission in our four-legged friends. The client with a "flat back" may be putting out, all unconsciously, a fairly permanent display of submission.

   "Oh, you bodyworkers, you think everything in the body has a psychological meaning!" Well, yes, we do, actually, and it is surprising how often it works out to be so. I've seen it go both ways, in fact -- get the attitude and the body assumes the corresponding posture, or vice versa, get the posture, surprisingly, and the attitude will follow. Don't believe me? Try this little experiment: For the next few minutes, sit with a "depressed" posture -- chest pushed down toward the belly, slumped, head forward, shallow breathing. We're not talking months here, just a few minutes, say, five. After these few minutes, notice your thoughts. Tending toward the dark side? Try being inspired (another pun, sorry). Try thinking light and happy thoughts. It's funny, but it works both ways -- body to attitude, or attitude to body. Germans use the same *haltung* to describe both inner and outer posture, much as we use "attitude."

2. **Bioenergetics: The Revolutionary Therapy That Uses the Language of the Body to Heal the Problems of the Mind.** (January 1994). Alexander Lowen, M.D.

The chronic muscular tensions blocking the free flow of excitation and feeling are frequently found in the diaphragm, in the muscles surrounding the pelvis and in the upper legs. Releasing them by using both a physical and a psychological approach makes people begin to feel "connected." That is their word. (pg. 88)

It should be clear from what I have said earlier that if the pelvis is immobile and rigidly held in a fixed position, it will prevent any pressure from above passing down and into the legs where it can be discharged. (pg. 240)

Tensions in the pelvic area are released through a variety of exercises and by massaging and kneading the tense muscles. A tense muscle can be palpated either as a knot or as a tight string. ... This book is intended to provide a general understanding of the intimate relation between personality and the body. (pg. 254)

3. **Joy**. (March 1996). Alexander Lowen, M.D.

   I started my therapy with Reich under the illusion that I was okay, but it did not take me long to discover that I was in fact frightened, insecure and physically tense in my body. (pg. 5)

   The path was the surrender to the body. What I had to surrender was my identification with my ego in favor of an identification with my body and its feelings. (pg. 5)

   Like most individuals in our culture, my pelvis was locked by chronic muscular tensions and unable to move freely and spontaneously… (pg. 6)

4. **Way to Vibrant Health: A Manual of Bioenergetic Exercises**. (First published 1977. 3rd printing – January 2003). Alexander Lowen, M.D. and Leslie Lowen

   <Obviously, the exercises described in *Way to Vibrant Health* should only be performed under the direction of a qualified Bioenergetic therapist. I am mentioning this book here for informational purposes only. The point is that there are specific exercises and when these are performed under the guidance of a trained bioenergetics therapist, then you will experience the releasing of long-held tensions and greater connection with the body.>

16

Conclusion

My Wujifa instructor likes to tell this story: There are many paths up the mountain. When you get to the top, you will find the immortals laughing and singing and arguing about which path was the best. The path that gets you to the top of the mountain is the path that is best for you.

I tried the "Qi" path for many years and found that this path led me to a dead end. I looked for another path. I'm finding that the path of developing deeper, internal kinesthetic feeling and fascial connection as outlined in the Wujifa curriculum is taking me much further along. Of course, because of all my "weights" and resistances, getting to the top of the mountain is taking me a long time. It might be that younger practitioners without such a desire to hold onto long-worn bad habits and routines might make quicker progress.

I attended a Chen Silk Reeling seminar with Grandmaster Chen Xiaowang years ago. (Grandmaster Chen Xiaowang is the 19th Generation Lineage Holder of Chen Family Taijiquan.) I was fortunate to have him adjust my posture so I could experience the feeling of "Qi flowing". With a slight adjustment to my elbow, I experienced "Qi flowing". With another adjustment, "Qi not flowing". And with another adjustment, again, "Qi flowing". From this I learned that when it comes to feeling connection there is no 30%, 80%, etc… of Qi flowing. The connection is either there or it isn't. It's like an On-Off switch. And having someone set me up to feel that connection is not the same as me finding and demonstrating it on my own. I have yet to demonstrate this on my own. I can achieve hints of connectedness but it is hard work to change my body from its patterns of blockages to one which is freely and fully connected.

The trickiest part of all is figuring out the feeling because there is nothing to mentally figure out. Attempts to mechanically produce it have taken me in the wrong direction. It is found in softness but it is not the softness. It feels like a stretch but it is not found in muscular stretch. Physical-emotional holding patterns, fascial adhesions, muscular scars, knots, chronic spasms etc. must be resolved to a certain level so the body can move freely which allows body alignment to be meticulously adjusted in a particular way and then after all this, one day "it" just shows up and the only words to describe it are those that are inadequate to describe it. And then the trick becomes how to reproduce that which I couldn't actually control the manifestation of in the first place. How did Yoda say it? "Do or do not. There is no try."

I've heard it said that finding the door is the trickiest part but once you go through the door, then it's easier to find the door the next time, and the next...

Of course, there are many aspects besides the pelvis that must be addressed and resolved on the path of developing internal strength. However, ignoring the pelvis is not the way to go either. Getting comfortable with relaxing the pelvis needs to become as natural as getting comfortable with relaxing the shoulders and working on alignment. However, getting comfortable with the idea, much less actually working with this area of the body can be a hurdle in itself! Yet, if you can get over these hurdles, the payoff in terms of the level of whole-body relaxation you can achieve will be a huge step forward!

When I practice my Wujifa zhan zhuang, and when I notice my mind wandering and thinking and tensing, I will shift focus to relaxing the anus (tension in the perineum and anus has co-arisen with thinking) and immediately I feel my entire pelvis relaxing and "widening" and somehow this feeling transmits up and into my shoulders and I feel my shoulders relaxing and "widening". Everything is all connected.

You may have heard the saying amongst Chen Taiji practitioners, "When one part moves, all parts move". This can also mean, when one part is stuck, then all parts are stuck. Due to the size of the pelvis and the centrality of its function in our bodies, having tension there is a huge impediment to getting all parts to move! So for me, relaxing and getting movement in and through the pelvis is a key component in achieving

Conclusion

"When one part moves, all parts move". I must be able to relax and move *ALL* parts of my body and not just the parts that can be discussed in polite social settings. I must be able to relax and move *ALL* parts of my body and not just the parts that I'm emotionally comfortable relaxing and moving. What we're aiming for is to achieve: When one part moves, then truly, *ALL* parts are able to move.

Again, if you have not or currently are not engaged in some effort to reconnect and get movement in and through the pelvis, you may have discovered your Achilles Heel in your development. And if some reason or emotion came up while reading this little book that will prevent you from engaging in working with your pelvis... Congratulations! You have discovered your first blockage, your first hurdle that you need to work on so you can move into relaxing and feeling into and developing a kinesthetic sensitivity in and through your pelvis, your center, your dantian, so you can round the crotch, so you develop better ground path, so you can develop whole body connection , peng, and...

Got it?

Appendix A

References to Crotch, Waist, Hips in Martial Arts

In this section, we will look at both the American and Chinese references to the crotch, waist, and hips in the martial arts. As you will see, references abound however it is only in the extraction, collection and presentation that we come to realize just how many people are talking about the importance of this area of the body.

I strongly encourage you to follow the links provided and read the entirety of these articles. The authors whose works I have excerpted have so much more to say than what I've provided here. Consider these excerpts as a "taste" of the fuller article.

Excerpts from Books and Articles in English

Martial arts in general talk about the need to move from the center. Even though different styles use the hips and waist differently, getting students into their pelvises sounds like it is a common problem. This is no less true in the internal martial arts.

The Chinese internal martial arts and qigong use their own language to describe different areas of this part of the body. For example, the lower abdomen is referenced by the dan-tian, (丹田; dāntián) the hip or inguinal crease is referenced by the kua (胯 kuà), the crotch is the dang, and the pelvic floor or perineum includes acupuncture points CV1 hui-yin (會陰; huìyīn) and GV-1 chang-qiang (長強; chángqiáng).

In my earlier Tai-chi days, I really didn't understand Chinese terms like "move from the dan-tian" from a western, anatomical perspective. Instead, I tried to force myself to imitate a sort of quasi-mystical, Chinese philosophical understanding of what this might mean. Through years of experiences and training, I've come to a more grounded and functional understanding of what is meant by pelvic-centered movement. I completely overlooked this basic functional aspect when I was wrapped up in dan-tian talk.

The reason I mention this is that in my early years, I read many of the below referenced books from that frame of reference. As I re-read these books for inclusion in this book, I see them now in a completely different light. I've learned that my frame of reference acts as a filter which embellishes the meaning I derive.

Function and Usage of the Kua: Q & A with Chen Zhonghua.
Posted by Editor on July 20, 2006
http://internalartsia.wordpress.com/2006/07/20/function-and-usage-of-the-kua/

The better you are at using the kua, the better your body is coordinated. So it will appear that different masters use the kua differently, with varying levels and depth of experience of that function. Ability to connect the kua with better integration with the body reveals higher skill.

In terms of function, it is better to emphasize the primary role of the kua, rather than the waist. On the surface, people view Tai Chi exercise in terms of the waist. Waist is what you see, but the work is done by the kua.

Appendix A: References to Crotch, Waist, Hips in Martial Arts

Distinguishing the Hip and Waist by Sam Masich
http://www.embracethemoon.com/perspectives/hip_waist.htm

There is perhaps, no greater stumbling block to the mastery of Taijiquan, than the murky confusion we are greeted with when we first begin a conscious study of the hips and waist. Virtually nothing in our western physical education prepares us for the study of this region.

Warriors of Stillness Vol. I: Meditative Traditions in the Chinese Martial Arts. (1997). Jan Diepersloot

When people first start learning, the lumbar spine, pelvis, and abdomen are often so frozen and locked in position that giving them instructions to maintain "tuck and suck" constantly only increases the general level of tension and inability to feel in the area. (pg. 56)

Cheng Hsin: The Principles of Effortless Power. (1999). Peter Ralston.

You must loosen the pelvis so that the energy can sink down into the legs and feet and accept the weight. When you relax and sink while standing, your legs will feel as if they are carrying more weight than usual and the feet will feel an increase in pressure against the earth. (pg. 13)

Open the pelvis

The entire pelvic structure should be loosened. The pelvis is an area most people keep tight and immobile. Because of its nature and usual lack of use, it is easy to overlook. The muscles are large in and around it, and difficult to loosen unless you "get in touch" with them. Because most people don't know they hold their pelvis, it is hard for them to relax it. When the pelvis massively relaxes for the first time, it is astounding. The whole area seems literally to drop, and you suddenly feel more grounded and in your feet. (pg. 26-27)

Restriction in the pelvis is the cause of many disabilities; holding the pelvis improperly or tightly causes severe problems and severance in many other areas of the body. The way you hold yourself, for example, is affected directly by the state of the pelvis. The inability of the knee to point with the toe is most often the result of a tight hip joint. The feet turning outward, or riding on one part instead of evenly, is frequently solved by relaxing the pelvis. (pg. 27)

Zen Body-Being: An Enlightened Approach to Physical Skill, Grace, and Power. (2006). Peter Ralston, Laura Ralston.

People often carry their weight too high up in the body and don't allow it to drop down toward the ground. It is pinched off, so to speak, at some point in the structure, frequently at the pelvis or in the legs. (pg. 94)

The Dao of Taijiquan: Way to Rejuvenation. (1989). Jou, Tsung Hwa. Edited by Lori S. Elias, Sharon Rose, Loretta Wollering.

Method 6: Rounding the groin or *diaodang* (吊裆). The lower the area of the body controlling the movement, the more relaxed the upper parts of the body, thereby preserving maximum stability. Thus for shifting the body weight, focus from your feet up your legs and then to your body. Furthermore, have the intention to keep the space between the legs rounded, the pelvis tucked under (so that the buttocks do not protrude outward) and the lower abdomen a little bit forward and upward. (pg. 170)

The crotch between your legs must be rounded so that the chansijing can develop in your legs. (pg. 213)

Appendix A: References to Crotch, Waist, Hips in Martial Arts

The Essence of T'ai Chi Ch'uan: The Literary Tradition. (1993). Benjamin P. Lo, Martin Inn, Susan Foe, Robert Amacker.

The motion should be rooted in the feet, released through the legs, controlled by the waist, and manifested through the fingers. (pg. 21)

The thirteen postures should not be taken lightly; The source of the posture lies in the waist. (pg. 63).

If there is any uncoordinated place, the body becomes disordered and weak. The defect is to be found in the waist and legs. (pg. 74)

3. *Sung* (relax) the waist. The waist is the commander of the whole body. If you can *sung* the waist, then the two legs will have power and the lower part will be firm and stable. (pg. 85)

Training Tip #1: The Components of Relaxing. (1993). *Internal Strength: A Practical Approach to Internal Strength and Qi.* Mike Sigman. Message posted at http://ismag.iay.org.uk/issue-1/training-tip.htm

Relaxation, or sung, does not imply limpness, or even no-strength. For instance, just in holding normal stances beginners are heard to howl after short time spans… more advanced students, whose leg strength has grown to accommodate their stances, stand relaxedly and claim that they are relaxed… but their legs are stronger. Even more advanced students, who have developed not only leg strength, but also a skill in the use of body angles, will find that their joints (the sinews) have become the load bearers, and the need for muscle tonus declines. True relaxation follows this line of development.

Training Tip #6: Using the Waist. (1994). Internal Strength: A Practical Approach to Internal Strength and Qi. Mike Sigman. http://ismag.iay.org.uk/issue-6/training-tip.htm

In the internal arts, the idea of "straightening the back" and "tucking the pelvis" (or "tucking the buttocks") is often mentioned. The problems begin to occur if too much tension is used in holding the pelvic tuck.

When the internal martial arts stress "relaxation," they don't mean "relax everything but the pelvic area and the back"... the slight pelvic tuck is a product of relaxing the lower back ("relax the waist") and relaxing the supporting knee(s). Often you hear long-term students complain of back problems because some teacher taught them to forcibly hold a pelvic tuck.

By relaxing the waist, while allowing a pelvic rotation (relax the knee!), we accomplish several things. First, the supporting and energy-storing abilities of the lower back are enhanced because the lumbar vertebrae come away from the lordotic curve and assume a more columnar configuration.

Secondly, a relaxed waist allows the hip joint(s) to easily assume a position in which the support of the ground's strength (peng) is readily transmitted through the hip, i.e., the hip and inguinal region (kua) are "open."

A rigidity on the upper side of the hip can be disadvantageous for the same reason, so the hip joint should always be "sunk" or relaxed; transmission of the ground strength is primary.

Appendix A: References to Crotch, Waist, Hips in Martial Arts

Authentic Xing Yi Quan. (2012) .Gong Zhong Xiang, Franklin Fick.

When you relax the Kua it needs to be comfortable and steady. The Dang Bu (Crotch Area) can not be separated too wide or too narrow. After practicing for a while the Qi and blood should be flowing freely. Then you should practice slightly contracting the Kua, which means contracting the joint and tendon slightly inward. (pg. 90)

Ti Gang (Lift the Anus) means to consciously contract the anal sphincter muscles and lift upward like you are holding in a bowel movement. Control your buttocks from sticking out too much to maintain the straightness of your tail bone, waist, and lumbar spine. The chest and stomach should contract inward. Qi sinks to the Dan Tien. (pg. 91)

In general when you practice Xing Yi Quan you must achieve: head pushes up, neck straight, chest contained and back lifted, wrist bends and palm props up, relax the shoulder and sink the elbows, sink the waist and straighten the spine, tuck the buttocks and lift the anus, Kua relaxed / loose and tight, abdomen solid and full, hook and lift the knee, agile stepping, steady steps, the front foot has to step with power, the back foot has to push with power, the three tips line up, the whole body naturally relaxed, and the upper and lower limbs in total coordination. (pg. 91)

9. Anus
When the anus is tightened the Qi can reach the four endings. The two sides of the pelvis have winding power and the buttocks connects them internally. When the posture is too low the power is diminished, therefore it is preferred to be higher. (pg. 296)

On Stance, Kua (Hips) and Dang (Crotch). Tu-Ky Lam.
http://tukylam.freeoda.com/egroup4.html

Kua in Chinese means hips. In Taijiquan, our waist and hips have to be relaxed and loosened. There is an excellent explanation for this requirement in the June 2003 issue of *Tai Chi* (page 14), which says "relaxing the kua is to allow the hips to set in their sockets (Note: my understanding of this is "relaxing our hips is to allow our buttocks to set in their sockets") Only then can the qi flow down from the body to the legs and your feet. It helps to give your feet the foundation of your strength. Then your qi will build up throughout your entire body". This is something all Tai chi students have to train to achieve, but easier said than done. You need to train correctly from 700 to 1000 hours (one hour a day for two or three years) to achieve this.

Dang means crotch, the place where our legs fork the body. Our crotch has to be round like an arch, not pointed like a capital A. When our crotch is round, we can shift weight and so move more freely.

Chen Style Taijiquan: The Source of Taiji Boxing. (2001). Davidine Sim, David Gaffney. (pg.62-65)

Tailbone, Buttocks, Kua and Dang.

Kua is the muscle on both sides at the inguinal crease at the top of the legs. ... The *kua* facilitate co-ordinate upper and lower body movements.

When the *kua* are relaxed, the weight burden on the legs increases. If the legs are not strong enough, as is common with beginners, it is easy to tighten up the *kua* resulting in the knees extending over the toes, abdomen and chest sticking out, and the body leaning backward.

Appendix A: References to Crotch, Waist, Hips in Martial Arts

Dang (the crotch) should be held open and rounded to ensure agile footwork and smooth shifting of weight. It should be held in an upside-down U shape, and not an angular V shape. This is the area where the *Huiyin* point is situated, where the *Du* and *Ren* channels begin. The point should be kept light and without tension, in order to create balance.

Kua and *dang* work closely together. To round the *dang*, the *kua* need to be relaxed and open; the muscles on the inner thigh have the feeling of slightly pushing back and out. During movement, there is a close relationship between the waist and *dang*, and between the *dang*, the *kua* and the knees. The waist is relaxed and sunk down, *kua* are opened, and knees are drawn in – leading to a naturally open and rounded *dang*.

Chen style's requirement of the rounded *dang* is strict. It should also be light, relaxed and flexible. Avoid the angular, rigid and collapsed *dang*. Collapsed dang is when the buttocks drop below the level of the knees. This locks the knee joints, making weight change awkward and footwork clumsy. The angle of the bent leg should not be less than 90 degrees. The *dang* area plans an important role both in the form movement and in usage. Keeping the *dang* rounded and opened increases strength in the legs.

COMMON MISTAKES:
Sticking out the buttocks – a sign of insufficient strength in the waist and legs to support the upper body.

Pushing the kua forward – this is considered a major problem. The top of the thigh is kept too rigid or too straight, is unable to sink down, and therefore prevents the waist from moving freely.

Collapsing the dang – when the dang is allowed to drop below the level of stability, i.e., below the level of the knees.

Not opening the dang sufficiently – resulting in an angular rather than a rounded dang.

Opening the dang too much – while opening the dang, the knees and the feet should be kept slightly drawn in, thus containing the energy and maintaining balance. (pgs. 64-65)

The knees do not bend independently, but in response to the *kua* relaxing, hips sitting and the tailbone extending. (pg. 66)

Combat Techniques of Taiji, Xingyi, and Bagua: Principles and Practices of Internal Martial Arts. (2006). Lu Shengli and Zhang Yun. (pg. 137-139)

Song yao – relax the waist: *Song yao* is one of the most important key points because it involves your waist, which is the center of your body and the locus of control for all your movements. If your waist is tight, you will not be able to relax any other part of your body. Your qi will not be able to move smoothly throughout your body, your internal force will not be sustained, your arms will not be flexible, and your footwork will not be nimble.

Guo dang – curve and expand the crotch: In *guo dang*, the arch formed by the inside surfaces of your legs and your crotch should expand and maintain a curved shape. This will help your *qi* sink and move smoothly down to your legs without becoming dissipated. *Guo dang* will also increase your root and the power in your legs. It will make your whole body very nimble.

Liu tun – tuck the buttocks under the lower back: *Liu tun* means that you must keep your lower spine straight so that your buttocks do not protrude. This movement will allow your waist to remain relaxed and your *shen* to rise.

Appendix A: References to Crotch, Waist, Hips in Martial Arts

How to Align Your Body For Better Qi Flow: A Guide to the Correct Practice of Taijiquan. (2003). Tu-Ky Lam.
http://tukylam.freeoda.com/practiceguide.html

The crotch is where your legs join or fork your body. It should be kept round like an arch so that you can turn or shift your weight easily. It can help you step forward (or backward) and yet can retreat quickly if need be. That is to say it help you have the insubstantial in the substantial and the other way round.

The Eight Skills of Taiji. (2008).
http://tcmdiscovery.com/Taiji/info/20081212_11497.html

The crotch is the perineum of the body. The baihui acupuncture point at the crown of the head must correspond to the perineum acupuncture point. This is necessary to keep the energy stream flowing freely to the top and the bottom.

The crotch must be round and solid. When the hips are apart and the knees turned slightly inward, the crotch is naturally round. If the knees are opened slightly, the thighs close inward and the hips separate a bit, the crotch is still round. When the perineum is raised slightly, the crotch is naturally solid. When the waist is relaxed and the buttocks tucked in, there will naturally be power from the crotch. Once the crotch has power, the lower limbs become even stronger and the standing steps steadier and firmer.

Small Frame of Chen Style Taijiquan. (2002, September). Jian Ge.
http://www.chinafrominside.com/ma/taiji/xiaojia.html
II. THE CHARACTERISTICS OF "SMALL FRAME" OF CHEN STYLE TAIJIQUAN

#3 Footwork (Bu Fa)

Because of the requirement to open hips and round the crotch, both feet should be kept parallel to each other, and never placed with toes pointing outwards (in the shape of letters "V" or "T"), otherwise the hip joint will not fold and crotch will lose its curve (and will take shape of "V" letter - so-called "sharp crotch" - and hence the requirement of rounding the crotch will not be met);

#6 Strength Method (Jin Fa)
Crotch shall open and be round, should not twist (Niu) or sway to the left and right horizontally (Shuan)". Bottom should relax and spread out to both sides, so that hips "wrap" (as if trying to embrace a big ball with legs), hip joint is kept tucked in (hips are folded), opening (Kai) at the rear and closing (He) at the front, so that the crotch becomes round;

What Are the Body Requirements of Tai Chi? Chen Village site. http://www.chenvillage.com/what-are-the-body-requirements-of-tai-chi

The most basic requirement for doing Tai Chi is song kua, or relax the hips, means that the muscles surrounding the hip joint, i.e. where the thigh bone meets the hip, should not be used to any great degree in supporting your structure. These hip muscles can then be used to adjust the angle of your pelvis so that your upper body can remain relaxed, or direct the jin if so required. If you haven't achieved a song kua, then everything else is academic. You will not be able meet the requirements for the rest of your body.

Basic Tips for Zhan Zhuang and the Pelvis. (2009). Richard J. Taracks. http://wujifaliangong.blogspot.com/2009/06/basic-tips-for-zhan-zhang-and-pelvis.html

The first point I'd like to share is that many people carry a lot of tension in the glutes or more simply said the butt muscles. When people have a normalized patterning of tension that is carried in the glutes you will find that the femoral heads are pulled back and twisting the legs so they often stand in daily life with their toes angled slightly outward.

The second pointer is also very common in so many people and that is the muscles found in the lower back area are shortened and tight. Some of these seemingly normal imbalances are found in these muscles and fascial groups: Erector spinae, Thoracolumbar fascia, Latlissimus dorsi muscle, Petlit's, Gluteal aponeurosis, Quadratus lumborum, Psoas, just to name a few.

What we aim for in the Wujifa standing practice skill set is to repattern or build in a more open responsive posture. We do this in learning to relax and adjust accordingly. Often is the case found in hip adjustments and relaxing the glutes and lower back muscles so the pelvis can shift and adjust to a more functional space for example in the standing practices.

Chen Family Taijiquan Tuishou (太极拳推手技法陈式). 1998. Wang Xi-an (王西安). Translated into English by Zhang Yanping. (2009). Australia: INBI Matrix Pty Ltd.

See "Chapter Five: Practices for the Buttocks and Crotch". pgs. 157-167.

5.1 Practices for the Buttocks
5.1.1 Overview
The requirements for positioning the buttocks in Taijiquan practice are very strict. (pg. 158)

Taijiquan novices sometimes err on over-gathering or raising the buttocks, which can result in various negative effects. (pg. 158)

5.2 Practices for the Crotch (Dang)

The shift between emptiness and solidity of the *Dang* area is used as a measure to monitor and adjust movement and speed of movement, and also serves as the key point to increase the power to be exploded. (pg. 160)

In the same way that the positioning of the Dang is very precise, the positioning of the anus also needs careful attention. (pg. 161)

Yuan Dang refers to the opening of the *Dang* area in a circular shape, when the distribution between the weight-bearing leg and the other leg is at a ratio of 3:7 or 4:6. (pg. 161)

<Note: the 3:7 or 4:6 ratio refers to the percentage of weight distribution in each leg.>

Hence, *Yuan Dang* reinforces the foundation and allows flexible body rotation in any direction.

5.2.3 Ding Dang – Tight Crotch

Ding Dang refers to a common mistake made by novice practitioners whereby one leg supports the body without relaxing. (pg. 162)

Ding Dang arises when the area connecting the weight-bearing right leg to the crotch remains tight. If a practitioner is advised to relax, he or she will typically re-distribute weight between the legs to a ratio of 5:6 or 5:5, which means there will not be opening-closing power if he or she crouches in the Horse Stance. This should be corrected at the earliest stages of learning. (pg. 162)

5.2.4 Jian Dang - - - Sharp Crotch

In *Jian Dang* position, the *Dang* area is shaped like an inverted "A", the bottom tip of the *Dang* area is tight and not relaxed. In this case, *Dang* cannot be lowered during routing and Tuishou practice and *Yuan Dang* cannot be formed at all. … This mistake may be tolerated in the old and weak if their aim is just to improve health, but cannot be ignored by younger practitioners who want to improve combat skills. ... If the habit of Jian Dang is allowed to form over a period of time, practitioners will become used to it and feel comfortable in this incorrect stance, which should be avoided. (pg. 163)

5.2.5 Tang Dang

Tang Dang happens when the legs are spread too far apart, out of proportion to the weight distribution required on the legs and lowered *Dang*. ... This situation is also called Ta Dang, meaning collapsing Dang. (pg. 164)

Typically, practice methods for Taijiquan routines start from large circle movements to smaller ones, then from smaller circles to no-circle movements. However, the opposite is true for Dang practice, which starts with smaller scale movements, growing to larger-scaled practice. (164)

The Illustrated Canon of Chen Family Taijiquan (太极拳图说陈式). 2007. Chen Xin (陈鑫). Translated into English by Alex Golstein. 2007. Australia: INBI Matrix Pty Ltd.

(About the author: Chen Xin (1849-1929) is the 16th generation descendant of Chen style Taijiquan. He spent 12 years (1908-1919) writing what has become a classic book detailing the theory and practice of Chen family Taijiquan. The original publication date is not known. This book has been published by Kaifeng Enlightened bookstores (开封开明书局) since 1933. Today it is reprinted by the Shanxi Science and Technology Publishing House (山西科学技术出版社).) http://translate.google.com/translate?hl=en&sl=zh-CN&tl=en&u=http%3A%2F%2Fwww.amazon.cn%2Fdp%2FB007ZLOOUO%3Ftag%3Dstt1-23

The crotch area is at the root of both thighs and must be opened. The size of this opening is not to be taken literally. If opened with conscious effort, even a tiny crack the width of a silk thread will suffice; without it, even a width of *3 chi* would not be sufficient to open the crotch. (pg. 245)

There are ten errors commonly made in the *Xia-bu Kua Hu* posture:
(3) when both feet are placed too close to each other, it is almost impossible to open the crotch;

(4) if the transverse distance between the feet is correct but the toes of both feet turned outward, the crotch area will <be> too inflexible for the body to 'sit down';

(5) 'sitting down' and digging into the ground too abruptly and rigidly could disengage energy at the top of the head from its connection with the energy of the rest of the body, leading to a diminished ability to lead it. This results in the crotch area becoming too opened and stiff. In this case, 'stiff' implies 'dead' while 'dead' signifies immobility, immobility means ineffectiveness and ineffectiveness indicates that the whole process is running in an uncertain and unstable way; (pg. 730)

(10) if waist and crotch energy sink down well but the energy of the buttocks and thighs cannot flow up, this means that the upper and lower body is not engaged in the entire mechanism of qi flowing. Hence the soles of the feet become weakened and easily knocked down by external forces.

All these ten errors may manifest in any of the posture's movements, at any level, physical or energetical. (pg. 731)

Appendix A: References to Crotch, Waist, Hips in Martial Arts

Sink the waist energy down, otherwise, the soles of the feet will become disconnected from the crotch energy, and become weak and unstable. (pg. 742)

In contrast, a properly opened crotch can help accumulate energy in the buttocks, which then flows to the lower abdomen to be released. When the lower abdomen is positioned correctly, the crotch will open itself properly – the opening will be narrow like a thread, and provide the appropriate emptiness and roundness to create a full energy connection between both sides internally. In comparison, a crotch opened to widely, that is, wider than the Chinese character for 'man', has a negative effect on the work of the arms. Generally speaking, when the upper body is narrow but the lower body wide open, the problem of a 'bottleneck' is created since the body is neither empty nor round. Though the lower body may be 'opened', this 'opening' is not effective. Hence the function of the crotch is to open the narrow pass between the upper and lower body. (pg. 736)

The Internal Athletics by Tommy Kirchhoff. Retrieved February 26, 2013 from http://www.futaichi.com/IntAth.html

Fu Wing Fay (1913-1993) said, "Yao (the waist) is the Lord of the body. Kua (the hips) is the hub center between the upper half and the lower half of the body. If you cannot loosen the waist and hips, your body will become as stiff as a stick, and fall with one blow. If you cannot loosen your hips, the upper and lower halves of the body cannot turn easily, and your chi cannot descend to the soles of your feet (called Yong QuanXue). If you cannot "grow roots," the center of gravity of your body will not be stable."

Shotokan Karate Training. Japan Karate Association at Columbia University. Retrieved February 26, 2013 from http://www.columbia.edu/cu/jka/training.html

The hips are a crucial, yet oft-neglected component in executing karate techniques.

Thoughts on Hip Problems & Martial Arts. (2004, August 3). Robert Carver. http://www.budoseek.net/vbulletin/showthread.php?6415-Thoughts-on-Hip-Problems-amp-Martial-Arts

I guess the bottom line I would like for everyone to take away from this is; just because something feels like a groin pull, or a sciatic nerve that is acting up, doesn't mean that it is. If the pain persists, for heaven's sake, go to an orthopedic doctor and get a proper diagnosis. Better safe than sorry.

Double Hip. (2006, July 14). Charles C. Goodin. http://karatejutsu.blogspot.com/2006/07/double-hip.html

In order to develop power using your whole body, it is necessary to connect your upper and lower body through your core and koshi. Hip motion is an important aspect of generating and directing power.

When a student is stiff and not used to a rotary use of the hip (koshi), we will try all sorts of exercises to get him to loosen up and move his hips.

Vital Hip Work of Karate. Dave Lowry. Black Belt magazine, November, 1997, (pg. 22)

Nearly all our sports use power generated in the upper chest, shoulders and arms. The most frequent complaint from Japanese martial arts instructors is that the Western students tend to move from the shoulders rather than from the hips. One need only to

Appendix A: References to Crotch, Waist, Hips in Martial Arts

compare the silhouette of Arnold Schwarzenegger with that of a *sumo* wrestler to see the difference.

The Importance of Hips in Brazilian Jiu Jitsu. Tim Bruce. Retrieved February 26, 2013 from http://www.bjjweekly.com/blog/post/the-importance-of-hips-in-brazilian-jiu-jitsu

In terms of importance for Jiu Jitsu proficiency, be it in practice or competition, the hips are by far the one area that has the greatest impact on performance in the sport.

The one thing that does seem to be missing in the training of many Jiu Jitsu practitioners is exercises designed to increase hip flexibility and overall speed and strength. The hips are designed to move and rotate as a ball and socket joint in a circular manner in almost a three hundred and sixty degree range of motion. The more active we are and the more we practice stretching and strengthening our hips, the more mobility and power we will possess in them. When people ignore training these important joints, they allow their hip flexors and hamstrings to tighten up and shorten which will cause a decrease in their overall flexibility and range of motion in their hips, especially as they grow older.

When our hips loose flexibility, we may begin to over compensate other muscle groups such as the knees, legs and lower back and begin to slowly develop chronic injuries over time. This can easily be avoided by adding a few beneficial exercises to your training routine.

Aikido and Hips. (May 29, 2011). Bartek Gajowiec. http://gajowiec.blox.pl/2011/05/Aikido-and-hips.html

Koshi - hip and pelvic complex look like a basket into which we dump many different states of emotional and physical overloading. We very often hide there the most unspoken mysteries of life, tension related to duties we face every day etc. We may or we may not see that or even realise that but that is how it is in real. And that can be a reason why we cannot use our hips effectively. That may be a cause for lack of life in our hips, lack of energy and lack of feeling aikido to the full.

Aikido, Aikibojitsu, and the Structure of Natural Law. (Oct 1, 2010). John Thomas Read. Technical Aikido, (pg. 125-128) http://www.aikibojitsu.com/files/Kokyu-Ho_Excerpt_2.pdf

The focus in the lower abdomen is recognized and considered to be important in all martial arts.

But it is not something to be deliberately achieved by effort. It appears naturally when maximum extensional range exists in the spine. Many martial artists mistakenly project their 'hara' (vital center) forward while in the seated posture in the mistaken belief that such a projection will make them strong.

Use of the Hip in Tang Soo Do. (2007). C. Terrigno. http://www.tangsoodoworld.com/reference/use_of_the_hip_in_tang_soo_do.htm

Our late Great Grandmaster Hwang Kee devoted a considerable amount of space in his textbook to the "scientific use of the hip" in Tang Soo Do, so it is imperative that practitioners take the time to fully understand it and apply it early on in their training so as not to create bad habits that will later be difficult (and time consuming) to correct.

The challenge for students with no prior training is to overcome their natural tendency to use one part or area of the body more than or in opposition to the other(s). Men, because of their physical build and strength are prone to predominately using the upper body while

Appendix A: References to Crotch, Waist, Hips in Martial Arts

at the same time applying too much power, literally throwing themselves head first into the movements.

Bagua Linked Palms. (2009). Shujin Wang. Translated by Kent Howard and Hsiao-Yan Chen. (pg. 19)

Chapter 7 Basic Principles

Draw Together Lower Abdomen:
The dantian is a good place to accumulate Qi. Keep the lower abdomen empty so Qi can sink. This is not achieved by hollowing the abdomen but by turning the upper thighs slightly inward and dropping the coccyx, which draws the area in and down. This is also called embracing the belly.

Coccyx Upright:
From the neck to the tip of the coccyx you must be extended and erect. This will allow the spinal nerves to function normally during exercise and your reflexes will be unimpeded and lively.

Draw in Buttocks, Pull up Sphincter:
Relax the lower back from the waist to the coccyx. The coccyx will naturally tuck inward as the buttocks are drawn down. You should have the intention of lightly contracting the area between the anus and the genitals.

The Essentials of Ba Gua Zhang. (2007). Gao Ji-wu and Tom Bisio. (pg. 78)

3. The Hips and Buttocks
Keep the buttocks curved, and round with a feeling of the tailbone sinking under and lift the anus. This does not mean to tighten it, but to have a feeling of lifting it. This activates the ren and

du meridians, and prevents leakage of the Qi through the body's "lower orifices."

4. The Waist and Lower Back
The waist is relaxed so that it can turn freely and the lower back sinks and is slightly rounded with a sensation that the ming men point is pushing backward.

Liu Bin's Zhuang Gong Bagua Zhang: South District Beijing's Strongly Rooted Style. (2008). Jie Zhang. (pg. 114)

The buttocks tuck under, and you gently close the anus and perineum...

Bagua Swimming Body Palms. (2011). Shujin Wang. Translated by Kent Howard and Chen Hsiao-yen. (pg. 17)

Draw in buttocks, pull up perineum: relax the lower back from the waist to the coccyx. The coccyx will naturally tuck inward as the buttocks are drawn down. You should have the intention of lightly contracting the area between the anus and the genitals [the perineum]. However, if the sphincter is so tight as to block the anus, you will create turbid Qi.

Excerpts and Translations from Chinese Articles

The following section contains selected results of internet searches on Chinese search engines. Similar to the "sharing" that occurs in American websites, I found many of the below articles on different websites sometimes with different titles and attributions. Therefore, I cannot vouch for the accuracy of the authorship nor the original publication date. I did my best to find the earliest time-stamped article assuming that doing so led me closer to the original author and posting date.

Appendix A: References to Crotch, Waist, Hips in Martial Arts

I do not know anything about the experience of the authors I am quoting. The excerpts range from articles with identifiable authors affiliated with universities, to well-known teachers, to anonymous bloggers. I believe the value of these excerpts, regardless of the author, lies in the instruction and insight provided. Excerpts were selected to provide as broad yet focused an understanding as possible. Each excerpt is a kind of piece of the puzzle. Seeing each together provides a fuller understanding.

Internal martial arts speak of the dan-tian as being located two to three fingers width below the navel. Translations of dan-tian that likely come from Buddhist, Taoist, Qigong or New Age concepts include terms such as: elixir field, sea of qi, energy center, etc. What you may not know is that both contemporary and older Chinese-English dictionaries, for example the Revised American edition of R. H. Mathew's Chinese-English Dictionary originally published in 1931, and the American edition published in 1943, translate dan-tian as "pubic region"! This suggests to me that the dan-tian can include an area of the body lower than two to three fingers width below the navel.

So even though dan-tian has a specific location and meaning in the internal martial arts, for these translations I have opted to translate occurrences of the characters (丹田; dān tián) as "pubic region". There are two reasons for this: 1. To remove any mystical Qi sensibility that you may attach to this word, and in so doing, 2. To ground your understanding in a very tangible, physical area of your body.

In China, teachers admonish students to loosen the hips (松胯; sōng kuà) and round the crotch (圆档; yuán dāng). The typical understanding of hips and crotch is: the hip is the part between the waist and thighs, and the crotch is the middle area between the two legs.

Dictionary translations of kua (松) appear as thigh or hip. For beginners, we usually call "the hip" the area between the legs and waist. This includes the pelvis and its components; the sacro-iliac joint, hip joint, ligaments of the spine, etc... Because different schools have different interpretations of the kua (胯), speaking of the kua (胯) can be a source of confusion. It is beyond the scope of this book to delve into the many interpretations and understandings of this term. My hope is that as you read these excerpts, whatever your interpretation or understanding, you will glean some insights that will contribute to your practice and development.

Generations of Chen Style Taijiquan (世传陈氏太极拳) by Chen Xiaowang (陈小旺1984. See Chapter 4, "Chen Style Taijiquan Five Levels of Gongfu" (陈式太极拳的五层功夫).

<Note: There are various translations of the "Five Levels of Skill". See my blog article, "The Five Levels of Taijiquan" for more information: http://internalgongfu.blogspot.com/2012/11/the-five-levels-of-taijiquan.html >

第一层功夫。
First Level of Effort (Gong-fu)

学习太极拳要求立身中正，虚灵顶劲，松肩沉肘，含胸塌腰，开髋屈膝，达到心气下降，气沉丹田。

Learning Taijiquan requires the following principles: hold empty spirit upward strong, loosen the shoulder, drop the elbow, draw in the chest, collapse waist/lower back, open the pelvis, bend the knees, Qi from the heart has to drop and that Qi has to sink to the pubic region.

The Essential Training and Coordination of the Waist and Hips in Chen Style Tai Chi Chuan Practice
(腰部和臀部的基本训练和协调的陈式太极拳练习)
by Chen En, Sports Science Research, 2002-01, pg:86-71.
http://en.cnki.com.cn/Article_en/CJFDTOTAL-TYKY200201021.htm

Appendix A: References to Crotch, Waist, Hips in Martial Arts

(About the author: Department of Public Physical Education, Ji-mei University, Xiamen, Fujian, PR China. Chenjiagou Taijiquan Association Xiamen division president.)

裆要圆，圆而稳，两大腿根要开，裆开不在大小，意开裆即开，不会开裆者，腿岔得再宽也无用。

It's important that the crotch area be round and stable. The base of the thighs must open. It doesn't matter if the crotch is open big or small, if your intention is to open, then it's open. If you can't open the crotch, then even if you spread your feet far apart it's useless.

裆口要放宽撑圆，易使裆劲自动尾闾中正，这样裆劲就更足，从而可稳固桩步。

If the "crotch mouth" is relaxed and round then it's easy for the crotch power to automatically adjust the tailbone to center and straight. Once you get this, then this shaped crotch has much better strength, thereby you can have a stable and solid stance.

同时还应与腰部密切配合，塌腰时需含裆，活腰时需松裆，而拧腰发劲时需扣裆，这样上下盘才易合，内劲在周身各处才能沉着透达。

The waist and crotch should be closely coordinated. Relaxing the waist helps keep the crotch relaxed. When the waist is alive and the crotch is relaxed, when twisting the waist as in fa-jin, you need to draw in the crotch. When the waist and crotch are relaxed, then the top and bottom "plates" are easier to fit together (like stacking dishes). Internal strength is attained when the whole body is calm.

Taijiquan "Crotch": The Locus of Movement (太极拳"裆"部的运行轨迹) by Mr. Pang Daming (庞大明) 2008-9-13
http://www.cntjq.net/article-3881-1.html

(About the author: Mr. Pang Da-Ming (1957-) was born in Weifang City, Shandong Province. Graduated from Chinese Medicine Academic School. He is the Yang Style a fifth-generation descendant of Yang Taijiquan line, then he studied Yang style Tai-chi followed Fu-zongyuan, Fu Zhongwen, Zhao bin.

Mr. Pang-Daming is a deputy or the Secretary-General of the Han Dan city Taiji Association which is the branch of Chinese "Yongnian" International Taijiquan Association. He is also the senior adviser in the Taichi Research Association and on the freelance editorial board of "Tai Chi" magazine in China. He has published more than 40 papers in the journal "Martial Arts Fitness", "Wuhun", "Shaolin and Tai Chi", "Taiji".)

《杨禄禅太极拳拳谱》中指出："丹田就是太极，练丹田就是练太极，所以斯拳以练丹田为必要事"。"裆为会阴，会阴为丹田之府"。这就充分的说明了"裆"在太极拳中的重要性。只知道它的重要性还不行，要知道"裆"在练太极拳时的具体要求和运行轨迹才能在实际中练习与运用。

《Yang Lu Chan Taijiquan Boxing Chronicle》 pointed out: working with the pubic region is precisely what Tai Chi practice is all about. So in boxing it is necessary to train the pubic region. "The crotch is the perineum and the perineum is the pubic region which controls everything." This fully illustrates the importance of the "crotch" in Tai-chi. Only knowing the importance of it is not enough. You want to know the "crotch" through Taijiquan practice; how the specific requirements and locus of movement is in reality practiced and put to use.

Requirements and Specifications of Chen Taijiquan Practice

(练习陈氏太极拳的要求和规格的探讨) by Sun Jia-xiong (孙嘉雄). 2012-4-24. http://www.cntjq.net/article-11665-3.html

(About the author: Sun Jia-xiong was one of the earliest disciples of Chen Zhenglei and went on to found the first Taijiquan Association at Fengtai city in Anhui Province. He has done a lot of work promoting Chen Style Taijiquan. After returning to Shanghai, he worked diligently to promote the authentic Chenjiagou Taichi Chuan and Taichi sword in the Peace Park, and welcomed many boxing friends. His students grew from 7-8 in the beginning to more than 200 over several years. For a short video, see: 孙嘉雄老师陈氏太极拳表演*, Chen Taijiquan demonstration by teacher Sun Jiaxiong* http://video.sina.com.cn/v/b/65762106-1957855044.html *)*

一般松胯不太容易掌握，因为胯部放松，会增加下肢的支撑力量。

Generally, relaxing the hips is not easy to grasp. However, when you relax the hips, you will increase the power of the lower limbs.

所谓裆部即人体会阴部分，裆在运动中和技击方面都比较重要。陈氏太极拳要求裆部在练习中要松活、虚圆、扣合及开（不能过低成"荡裆"或过高成"尖裆"），这样气血容易流畅，运动时又稳又灵。

The so-called crotch, the perineum part of the human body, the crotch in sport and martial movement is of utmost significance. Chen Taijiquan requires crotch exercise to be relaxed, alive, hollow, round, drawn in and harmonized with open (Make sure that when you do this that you're not too low to be a "swing crotch" or too high to be a "pointed crotch".) so that qi moves easily and your movement will be stable and agile.

Using Crotch Techniques (运裆之技法) by Lin QuanBao or Lim Chuan Poh (林泉宝). 2007-08-06.
http://blog.sina.com.cn/s/blog_48b6934401000b1c.html

*(About the author: Wrote the book: Taijiquan Internal Strength Cultivation (*太极拳内功修*). 316 pages. For a short video, see:* http://www.56.com/u57/v_NDU1ODg4ODY.html *)*

练太极拳功夫主要的就是练"裆"。

The main practice of Tai-chi Chuan gongfu is training the "crotch".

太极拳活与不活，全在于裆的运作。裆不活，动作必然呆滞。裆胯是太极拳的天机。所谓"天机"者，玄机关窍之意，凡动作变化全凭于此。不得此中奥秘，难以练成太极功夫。

Whether Tai-Chi Chuan is alive or not depends on the full operation of the crotch. If the crotch is not alive, then movement will inevitably be sluggish. The crotch and hip is the secret of Tai-chi Chuan. This so-called "secret", means every change in action depends on this mysterious body opening. Without understanding this profound mystery, it is hard to imagine succeeding in training Tai-chi gongfu.

裆跨在太极拳中起着提纲挈领的作用，如何运作，很难用言语来表达。

It is very difficult to express in spoken language the essentials of the function and operation of the crotch and hips in Tai-chi Chuan.

Appendix A: References to Crotch, Waist, Hips in Martial Arts

"运裆"首先要看老师是如何启动裆胯的，如果连这一点细微之处也看不出来，那么就无法使自己走运裆圈，无法克隆这个裆启的源头，无法做到以裆代手的运作。

To learn "moving the crotch", you first must see how the teacher starts to move the crotch-hip. If you cannot see how the crotch moves, then you will not have luck making your own crotch round. If you can't see it, then you can't imitate it. But once you do get it, then seeing crotch movement is as obvious as seeing your hands move.

第一要掌握太极拳的要领；第二要练松至柔；第三要运裆，这是出内劲的关键；第四技法，没有技法不能与人交技，缺一不成。

First, you must know the main point of Tai-chi Chuan. Second, you must practice loose until soft. Third, you must move the crotch. This is crucial for internal strength. Fourth, you must have technique because without technique you cannot transmit technique and will never succeed.

Chen Style Taijiquan 18 Important Points of the 9 Sections (陈式太极拳九节十八要论) by Xu Hai-Liang (徐海亮). Chinese Wushu Magazine (中华武术), May 2012., pg. 54. http://2010.cqvip.com/QK/81606X/201205/42148088.html

*(About the author: Xu Hai-Liang co-authored the book "Chen Taijiquan Qigong" (*陈氏太极拳养生功*) with Chen Zheng-lei (*陈正雷*)* Article reposted on http://www.taiji.net.cn/article-16101-1.html by Qing Fen Xuan (清风轩) 2012-5-17

练习陈式太极拳，要求开胯圆裆。开胯是指胯部关节和肌肉的感觉，而不是把两腿分开很大角度。圆裆是指大腿根部内侧要圆。开胯的同时又要圆裆，两者要同时兼顾、合二为一。要想达到这个要求，一定要在想象中把两条腿在裆、胯部位连成一体，形成一个拱形，即字母"n"的形状。这样，在行拳的过程中，无论如何拧转，只是在"n"的形状上发生变化，即使身法转换，也能保持外胯松而内裆圆，并使身体上、中、下三节浑然一体、周身一家。只有胯开裆圆，才能更加易于步法的进退和重心的变换。

Practicing Chen Style Taijiquan requires opening the hips and rounding the crotch. Opening the hips refers to the hip joint and feeling of the muscle without separating the two legs at a great angle. Round the crotch means to round the inner thigh. At the same time you open the hips you must also combine this with round the crotch. In order to meet this requirement, we must picture the two legs in the crotch, where the thighs meet the body and form an arch in the shape of the letter "n". Thus in the process of becoming an expert boxer, whichever way I turn, only the "n" shape changes. No matter which way you move, you still must keep the outside of the hip relaxed and the inside of the crotch round. Make the upper body, middle, and lower three as one, unified body. If the hip stays open and the crotch stays round, then your advance and retreat footwork as well as shifting your center of gravity will be easier.

Guo Yunshen's Secret Transmission of Xingyiquan Lower Power Stance (郭云深秘传形意拳下势桩) by Feng Yun Sheng (风云生). JINGWU magazine, April 2008, page 22-24.
http://wuxizazhi.cnki.net/Magazine/JWZZ200804.html

Appendix A: References to Crotch, Waist, Hips in Martial Arts

Article reposted on http://forum.sports.sina.com.cn/thread-541686-1-1.html (2008-12-16)

那么何为坐？一般初学者习惯将坐与蹲弄混，却不知过去的师爷在写谱时用字十分考究，坐与蹲是不一样的，蹲是下肢的动作是膝盖与腿的夹角变了，而坐是身体躯干的动作，腿上是没有变化的，

What does it mean to sit? Generally, the beginner customarily confuses sitting and squatting, and does not know the old masters elegantly described their study. Sitting and squatting is not the same. Squatting is the action of the lower limbs changing the angle of the knee and leg while sitting is in the movement of the torso. The legs do not change.

或者换一个说法，你不妨把坐胯的要求理解为下身要下沉下坐，而下肢双腿却欲起的这么个矛盾状态！

Or, in other words, you can think of the body wanting to sit down and at the same time the legs wanting to stand up. This is the feeling to find in this contradiction!

Theory of Taijiquan Four Ounce Push a Thousand Pounds (论太极拳之四两拨千斤) by Wu Qing-Zhang (吴庆章). 2007-12-10. http://blog.163.com/zhanglianwu_tj/blog/static/4251652620071110 95432918/ Published in JingWu Magazine, June 2009 by Mr. Sun Wan-Zhi (孙万智) http://mall.cnki.net/magazine/article/JWZZ200906028.htm

(About the author, Sun Wan-Zhi: Practicing martial arts since childhood. Currently a member of the Heilongjiang Province Suihua City Taijiquan Association and Vice President of Suihua City, Heilongjiang Province Wushu

Association. 11th generation heir Chen style small frame Taijiquan. Selected as a disciple of Master Chen Boxiang. For more information see: http://baike.taiji.net.cn/index.php?doc-view-1740.html)

一、"中正、松沉和圆裆"是练习所有太极功夫的基本要求，三要素环环相扣、作用非凡。失去中正的松就不能沉，不沉裆就不能圆，没有圆就没有撑，就蓄不了劲，所有功夫就失去基础。

First, "the principle of relax, sink and round the crotch" is the basic requirement when practicing Tai Chi kung-fu. If you have these three linked together then the effect is extraordinary. If you lose center-upright, then you cannot sink. If you cannot sink the crotch, then you cannot round. If you cannot round, then you will have no support. Then you cannot store strength because you have no foundation.

Fundamental Neijia Boxing Tactic: How to Round the Crotch! (内家拳中的重要之诀：怎样圆裆！) by blogger known as: "Martial Arts Masterpiece". 2009-05-06. http://blog.sina.com.cn/s/blog_5d9eeb970100d90k.html Reposted on http://www.taiji.net.cn/article-10962-1.html 2009-08-28.

内家拳，在洗练过程中，师傅总是强调"提肛"之重要！

The Neijia chuan masters always emphasized the importance of "lifting the anus" during training!

Round Crotch and Open Crotch (圆裆与开裆). Author known as "kangyongde" (2007-10-07). http://www.taijicn.net/html/92/t-6692.html

Reposted as: **Brief Talk on Taijiquan Crotch Circle** (浅谈太极拳的圆裆) by Li Zhen, in: Chinese Wushu Magazine, November 2012.
http://2010.cqvip.com/qk/81606X/201211/43728023.html
Also Reposted in: http://www.taiji.net.cn/article-18071-1.html
Repost Date: 2013-1-2

圆裆是太极拳的一个重要的要领，但裆部在生理结构的特殊部位，确实难以用可以让人去指点和现场纠正，定义的描述也确实让人把简单问题复杂

Round crotch is the main point of Taijiquan, but due to the particular place of the crotch in the physiological structure of this area, indeed it is hard to point to and correct this spot. Indeed the description of the definition allows people to complicate the simple.

圆裆的目的是为了让下盘符合力学的拱弧结构，古时候中国多拱型桥，人们造桥就是利用拱弧的原理。

The goal of round the crotch is to make the arc consistent with the mechanical structure of ancient China's multi-arch bridge. People built bridges using the principle of arches.

造桥前先做一个扇面的木架，然后从底部的两端呈半弧状排列垒石头，到中间合拢阶段的最后一块石头是在圆弧拱的顶点，也就是相当于人体的裆部，底部的两端就是好比人的两足。

Before building a bridge, first make a wooden frame in the shape of a Chinese fan, then stack the stones from the base of each side following the arc-shaped arrangement and set the last stone in the middle, the culmination of the circular arch. This is equivalent to the body: the two ends are the two feet and the apex is the crotch.

好的造桥师，垒石时不用灰浆，合拢最后的石头放上之后，拿开木架，大桥纹丝不动，原理就是能把力量传递到两端导如入地下。

Good bridge-building engineers can join stones without mortar. After the last stone is put in place and the wooden frame removed, the bridge remains motionless. The principle is to guide force to the ends into the ground.

所以中间的石头的大小就是影响到圆弧结构的合理。

Therefore, it is reasonable that the size of the center stone affects the arch's structure.

石头太大，也许就是故意的开裆撑裆，大桥没有应力，石头小了，就是尖裆和荡裆，架子就会散掉，即使肌肉钢精扯着，毕竟不是一顶合理的桥……

If the stone is too large, that is the crotch is too wide, the bridge cannot handle the stress. If the stone is too small, that is the crotch is too pointed, the structure will collapse. Even if refined steel is used (that is even if you use muscle to hold your structure together), in the final analysis, this is not a reasonable bridge.

The Role and Requirements of the Crotch in Taijiquan (太极拳裆的作用与要求) by Li Chun (黎春). 2009-5-16. http://www.cytjw.cn/bbs/forum.php?mod=viewthread&tid=6731

研究裆的作用与要求，不能孤立地看待，它是人体结构一个组成部分，与腿、脊、胯紧密相连，腰部旋转与它的转动是分不开的。

Appendix A: References to Crotch, Waist, Hips in Martial Arts

Study the functions and requirements of the crotch. It cannot be regarded in isolation. It is an integral part of human body structure and closely linked to the legs, spine, hips, waist rotation. These are inseparable.

如果裆部转动不灵，腰轴旋转的灵活性就势必受到影响，力由脊发就会受阻，发力大大减弱。

If the crotch movement is not flexible then the flexibility of waist rotation is bound to be affected. If the power in the spine is blocked then the ability to exert power is dramatically reduced.

How to Achieve the Round Crotch and Loose Hips? (怎样做到圆裆松胯？) by Tai-Chi Chuan Association of Harbin City: Publication Department. 2012-08. http://www.hrbtjq.com.cn/show.aspx?id=1735&cid=67

圆裆松胯是演练太极拳做到松沉的重要因素，是保证演练时立身中正的重要环节，是练习者容易忽视的要领。

Rounding the crotch and loosening the hips is a significant factor in practicing loose and relax in Tai-chi Chuan. This practice ensures standing centered and upright with significant connection. It is easy for practitioners to overlook these essentials.

Tai-chi Chuan Waist and Crotch Power (太极拳的腰裆功). Author unknown. 2008-5-30. http://www.cntjq.net/article-2565-1.html

然而有些人练习太极拳多年，却不知道用腰，更不懂得腰裆结合的妙用。

However, some people practice Tai-chi Chuan many years, but do not know how to use the waist/lower back, further still, they do not know the wonderful effect of connecting the waist and crotch.

太极拳对于裆部的要求是：圆虚松活。即两胯根与两膝盖撑开撑圆，又要有虚虚相合之意，裆虚圆则下盘有力，支撑八面；两胯放松则裆可松活，虚实转换也就轻灵快捷。

Taijiquan's requirements for the crotch are: round, hollow, relaxed, alive. The two knees together with the two hip-roots support the open and round. This looks like nothing but really is connected. If the crotch is hollow and round then the lower "plate" will be strong to support the eight directions. When the two hips relax, then the crotch can be relaxed and alive. The actual situation changes also soft, lively and quickly.

How to Practice Taichi Hips (如何练习太极胯). Author unknown. 2011-8-25.
http://blog.sina.com.cn/s/blog_8939ed470100tgjq.html

练太极拳要求裆要开，圆撑、虚撑、虚灵，实质上是对胯骨的要求，若要开裆，胯根必须松开撑圆。胯不开，裆为人字夹裆。既不能承受体重的重压，又不能使身体重心下降。

Taijiquan requires opening the crotch: round support, hollow support, calm mind. Essentially the requirement for the hip bone to open the crotch, the hip roots must release and round. If the hips do not open the crotch, then this creates a pinched ("A" shaped) crotch and this cannot support the weight of the body nor can the center of gravity drop.

Appendix A: References to Crotch, Waist, Hips in Martial Arts

初练时，可尽量放松臀部和腰部的肌肉。轻轻使臀肌肉外下方舒展，然后，再轻轻向前向里收敛。

Initially when practicing, try your best to relax the muscle of buttocks and waist as much as possible. Gently stretch the lower and outer gluteal muscles, gently moving and converging inward.

Taijiquan Explaining Seven Secrets: Loose Waist and Loose Hips (太极拳解密之七：松腰松胯)   Author unknown. 2012-1-16. http://iask.sina.com.cn/q/19529989.html

松腰：是方法，开跨：是目的。

Relaxing the waist is the method. Opening is the goal.

而人的腿，是由骨头和肌肉组成的，构成了支撑体，从人体的结构上看，骨头是支撑胯骨的边部的，也就是支撑在胯骨的外侧的尖端位置，但由于肌肉力巨大，造成肌肉支撑在前后裤线的内侧，掩盖了骨头的支撑，造成无法沉裆，也就阻挡了开跨。

While the person's legs are composed of bones and muscles, constituting the body's support, from the structure of the human body, the bones support the outside part of the hip bone. That is, support is at the highest position of the outer side of the hip bone. But because the muscle strength is huge, this causes the muscles to support around the inside of the trouser line (inseam), concealing the bone support, which causes an inability to sink the crotch, which then hinders "opening the door".

通过站桩，练拳等的练习，练的是大腿前部的肌肉，由于大腿前部练得肌肉力很强壮，就会慢慢造成大腿后部、胯部、屁股等的地方的大块肌肉慢慢放松，先是这些地方的肌肉放松了，大腿前部的肌肉力的面积加大了、也强壮了，这时，再慢慢放松大腿前部的肌肉的用力面积，这时就会造成前后裤线内的支撑点，慢慢的往大腿的骨头上转移，最终由骨头支撑住胯部，等于支撑的位置，由裤线的位置，转移到胯骨的外侧，而大腿前部用力的肌肉力，从而成为辅助的支撑。

Zhan zhuang and other boxing practices train the front muscle of the thigh to become strong. When the front of the thigh muscles are very strong, slowly this will allow the back of the thigh, hip, buttocks and large muscles to slowly relax. As these areas relax, the front thigh muscle strength increases and overall power increases. At this time, then slowly relax the muscles of the front of the thigh. At this time you will see results inside the trouser line support point. Slowly shift toward the thigh bone and finally reside in the bone support. The position of equal support occurs when transfer (weight bearing) to the outside of the hip bone. The front thigh muscle is strong and thus becomes auxiliary support.

由于支撑点转移到胯骨的位置了，支撑点远离中间，从而使得裆部能够下沉了，这就是沉裆。

As the support points transfer to the position of the hip bone, as the support points move away from the middle, then the crotch is able to sink. This is sink crotch.

Waist Thigh Theory (reprint) (腰胯论（转载）). Author unknown. 2009-12-22.
http://blog.sina.com.cn/s/blog_4b0df1270100h05r.html

Appendix A: References to Crotch, Waist, Hips in Martial Arts

Reposted as: Xingyiquan Waist and Hip Theory (形意拳腰胯论).
Author unknown. 2010-04-24
http://www.fushixingyi.com/Article_Show.asp?ArticleID=448

二、"合胯、圆裆"是形意拳对胯部规范的一组劲力。这组劲力也可以被称作"里撑外裹"劲，就是胯部（包括大腿）外侧要有向里合、向里裹的劲，而裆（包括大腿）内侧要有外撑的劲。这样胯部（包括大腿）的结构象拱桥一样，坚固而有弹性。这里特别要注意的是："里撑外裹"必须取得劲力上的平衡，不可显露于外，也就是不能尖裆或敞裆。

Second, the "together hip, round crotch" is a Xingyiquan hip specification that creates power. This combined strength can also be referred to as "the inside stays, the outside wraps" strength. This is hip (including thighs) outside and inside together, wrap around strength, and crotch (including thighs) inside to outside support. This shape hip (including thighs) has the structure of an arch bridge, strong and flexible. This special attention is: "the inside stays, the outside wraps" strength balance must be obtained, not exposed on the outside, also is not pointed crotch or too far open crotch.

The Waist-Thigh Vital Role in Tai-Chi Chuan (腰胯在太极拳中起着提纲挈领的作用) Author unknown.

http://www.cntjq.net/article-434-1.html Posted: 2008-5-29
Other sites where posted:
http://www.cntaijiquan.com/tjqyj/946.html
http://blog.sina.com.cn/s/blog_634355550100pmdf.html
http://www.taiji.net.cn/article-11842-1.html
http://www.cn-boxing.com/info/info_3281.html

放松腹股沟和会阴穴、松腰敛臀(亦俗称塌腰)对松胯圆裆亦起到较大作用。另外注意放松胯关节和臀部肌肉要放松，不能死顶骨盆，夹僵胯部。松胯起码要达到两个目的：一是轻灵，通过胯关节的肌肉韧带合理收缩舒张，胯关节的各骨关节能灵活转动，不产生辅助肌肉韧带做负功的现象；二是松腰沉稳，通过松胯更好地松腰，以身带领肢体内外运动，恰到好处地使意、气、劲合一，能使身体协调完整，松而不懈，沉而不僵。

Relaxing the groin and perineum, loosening the waist and restraining the buttocks (also commonly known as arched back) also plays a major role in loosening the hips and rounding the crotch. Moreover, pay attention to relaxing the hip joint. Relax the muscles of the buttocks and waist. The top of the pelvis cannot be rigid, pinched, stiff hip. Loosening the hips serves two purposes: one is achieving softness and agility through the hip muscle ligament with reasonable contraction and relaxed opening of each bone of the hip joint; flexible rotation. This should not produce auxiliary antagonistic muscle ligament work. Second, the waist is loose, sunk, and settled. Relaxing the waist improves loosening the hips which guides the body's inside and outside movement just right to create the feeling of unity, of whole-body coordination. Relaxed but not limp. Sunk but not stiff.

The Importance of Loosening the Waist and Opening the Hips in Taijiquan (太极拳松腰开胯的重要性). Author unknown. 2009-6-19. http://powersight.blog.sohu.com/118921143.html

胯是大拳头！全身是手手非手！

Hip is big fist! Whole body is hand-in-hand, not hand!

Appendix A: References to Crotch, Waist, Hips in Martial Arts

成人的盘骨，尤其是男人，已经硬化，其构合缝隙的软骨，也已钙化，连成一起，所以成年後才学太极，不易开胯，两年而能开胯，已经算快。

The adult pelvis, especially in men, has already hardened. The cartilage structures are calcified and joints are fused together and so adults learning Tai Chi do not find it easy to open the hips. Two years to open the hips is considered fast.

Appendix B

Qigong - Excerpts from Books and Articles in English

According to Qigong Fever: Body, Science and Utopia in China by David Palmer (2007), the word "qigong" was coined in 1949. Thus, the typical hyperbole that qigong is thousands of years old is technically not true. That said, there is a centuries old tradition of exercises known as Daoyin which the Chinese government "appropriated" from doctors, healers, and martial artists across China, stripped these exercises of their context and purpose and repackaged and mass marketed. This is what got exported and repackaged again in the U.S. and is what we came to know as qigong.

To get a sense of the historical purpose, use and evolution of Daoyin exercises, I suggest reading Chinese Healing Exercises: The Tradition of Daoyin by Livia Kohn (2008). What started as simple exercises for sedentary aristocrats later got appropriated by Taoist groups and assigned flowery language and mystical connotations. It's an interesting read.

Reading these two books should give you a fresh perspective on the carnival-like arm waving, feel-the-qi-between-your-hands practice that is common in the United States. However, getting below these superficial side-show exercises yields some interesting and deeper practices. Those which reference the pelvic floor are those which I have excerpted below.

The Essence of Taiji Qigong: The Internal Foundation of Taijiquan, Second Edition. (1998) Yang, Jwing-Ming. (pg 73).

Huiyun and Anus Coordination

The technique is very simple. If you are doing the Buddhist breathing, every time you inhale, gently expand your Huiyin and anus, when you exhale you hold them up gently. If you are doing the Daoist breathing, the movement of the Huiyin and anus is reversed: when you inhale you gently hold them up and when you exhale, you gently push them out. This up and down practice with the anus is called "Song Gang" (松肛) and "Bi Gang" (閉肛) -loosen the anus and close the anus. When you move your Huiyin and anus, you must be relaxed and gentle, and must avoid all tension. If you tense them, the Qi will stagnate there and will not be able to flow smoothly.

The trick of holding up and loosening the Huiyin and anus is extremely important in Nei Dan Qigong. It is the first key to changing the body from Yin to Yang and from Yang to Yin. The bottom of your body is where the Conception (Yin) and Governing (Yang) Vessels meet. It is also the key to opening the first gate,...

Qigong Meditation: Small Circulation. (2006). Yang Jwing-Ming. (pg. 227 - 228).

Through contraction and relaxation of the perineum, Qi can be regulated. If the anus is gently held up, the perineum tightens and seals the Qi gate. When it is gently pushed out, the perineum relaxes, and the Qi gate opens.

<Note: CV1 or *hui-yin* is considered one of the "Tricky Gates" (*xuan guan*); a key place in qigong training. See also page 390 of Qigong Meditation: Small Circulation. >

Appendix B: Qigong - Excerpts from Books and Articles in English

The Root of Chinese Qigong: Secrets of Health, Longevity, & Enlightenment. (1989, 1997). Yang Jwing-Ming.

However, as you get older and gradually lose the habit of this abdominal movement, the path becomes obstructed and the Qi circulation weakens. The most significant blockage can occur at the Huiyin cavity (Co-1;) (Figure 3.2). Try an experiment. Use one finger to press firmly at your Huiyin cavity while your abdomen is moving in and out. You will discover that the Huiyin cavity moves up and down in sync with the in and out motion of the abdomen. It is this up and down motion of the perineum which keeps the Huiyin cavity clear for Qi circulation. (pg. 39)

For example, when you were a child, the Huiyin cavity (Co-1;) (Figure 6-1) in the perineum was wide open. However, as you got older and abandoned abdominal breathing, it gradually plugged up so that the Qi circulation through it became sluggish. There are a number of other areas where the Qi path narrows and the circulation slows down. Wherever the circulation is sluggish and not smooth, the Qi supply to organs and entire body will lose its balance and you may become sick. (pg. 84)

Normal abdominal breathing is an important part of Buddhist Qigong training and so it is often called "Buddhist Breathing". To practice it, you must first use your Yi to control the muscles in your abdomen. When you inhale, intentionally expand your abdomen, and when you exhale, let it contract. In addition, when you inhale, you should gently push out your Huiyin (Co-1) cavity or anus, and when you exhale, hold it up. (pg. 129)

The Way of Qigong: The Art and Science of Chinese Energy Healing. (1999). Ken Cohen. (pg. 373).
<This excerpt refers to "Song Kua">

This expression is often combined with yuan dang "round the crotch", meaning relax the entire groin-genital region. The opposite of yuan dang would be to stand pigeon-toed with knees collapsed inward. This squeezes and compresses the crotch. Yuan dang is emphasized in Taiji Quan but not in all styles of qigong.

The Complete System of Self-Healing Internal Exercises. (1986). Dr. Stephen T. Chang. (pg. 93).
< in the section, "Instructions for the Male Deer Exercise" >

It is crucial to learn control over the anal muscles if one is to master the later meditative and breathing Internal Exercises. These muscles may be described as a door or a lock... It is essential then to gain mastery over this lock if one is to strengthen one's system sufficiently to begin to energize the spiritual centers in the body.

Dragon and Tiger Medical Qigong, Volume 1: Develop Health and Energy in 7 Simple Movements (2010). Bruce Frantzis. (pg. 209).

Keep your perineum open. The perineum is the area located between your anus and genitals. Closing the perineum diminishes the energy flow between your legs and torso...

Qigong for Treating Common Ailments: The Essential Guide to Self Healing. (2000). Xiangcai Xu.

Keep the waist and abdomen relaxed. The waist and abdomen are vital for proper training and guiding of Qi. The abdomen is usually

Appendix B: Qigong - Excerpts from Books and Articles in English

described as the furnace for refining vital energy. The waist is the residence of the kidneys (the repository of original Qi) and the gate of life (an energetic construct between the kidneys) and is therefore an important source or Qi and blood circulation. (pg. 13)

Place the feet a little wider than shoulder width, slightly contract the muscles of the legs with the knees pulling somewhat toward each other to round the crotch. (pg. 52)

Nei Dan Meditation Training. (07 Mar 2011). http://www.energygatesqigong.info/exercises-meditation/nei-dan-meditation-training.html

In Daoist breathing, the secret of bringing the Qi to the Weilu is to tighten the anus gently while inhaling. This is called Bi Gang (Close the Anus, M V-) in meditation. When exhaling, the anus is relaxed and Qi is guided to the Weilu. This is called Song Gang (Relax the Anus). This coordination should be done even after Small Circulation has been completed.

Six Breathing Practices. (July 12, 2008). Michelle Wood. http://bewellqigong.blogspot.com/2008/07/six-breathing-practices.html

b. Buddhist Breathing
Remember, you are gently holding up the Huiyin and anus, not tightening them. When you hold them up they can remain relaxed, but if you tighten them you will impede the Chi circulation. When you tense them you also cause tension in the abdomen and stomach, which can generate other problems. In the beginning, you will seem to need to use your muscles to do this, but after you have practiced for a time, you will find that the mind is more important than the movement of the muscles.

c. Taoist Breathing

When you are leaning Taoist Breathing, you should first stop your Huiyin and anus coordination until you can do the Reverse Breathing smoothly and naturally. Then resume the Huiyin and anus coordination, only now when you inhale you hold up your Huiyin cavity and anus, and when you exhale, you relax them.

Opening the Energy Gates of Your Body: Qigong for Lifelong Health. (Tao of Energy Enhancement). (2005). Bruce Frantzis.

(5) The Anus and Rectum

Dissolve as far up the anus as any blockage is felt, no more than a few inches deep. This is an extremely important gate, and is definitely helpful in relieving constipation, hemorrhoids, and preventing colon cancer. (pg. 72)

(6) The Perineum

Located between the genitals and the anus, the perineum is the point where energy from the legs and the body joins. (pg. 72)

If your body or mind experiences great difficulties when you practice Chi Gung, simply stop. The trouble may not reside in you, but rather in faulty teaching or your misunderstanding the instructions. (pg. 158)

The Great Stillness: The Water Method of Taoist Meditation Series, Vol. 2 (2001). Bruce Frantzis.

Taoists Emphasize Internal Feeling of the Body

… Taoists initially emphasize body practices that are based on actual feeling rather than on such purely mental processes as visualization. There are many in all cultures who essentially ignore

Appendix B: Qigong - Excerpts from Books and Articles in English

their bodies, who cannot actually feel the functioning of their bodies, and who live their lives totally in their heads. (pg. 33)

Taoists have always placed great significance on physical sensation and on directly experiencing the Consciousness locked inside the body... (pg. 33)

... a Taoist-like emphasis on making the body fully alive can be a beneficial counterbalance to humans becoming ever more physically numb and unaware. (pg. 33)

After you have gained an initial access to the sensations of your interior world by breathing or vibrating your insides, you can then practice by leaving these preliminary training aids behind and concentrating on using only your mind's awareness and intention to penetrate inside yourself. Normally, some people find it takes time (weeks, months, or even years of sustained practice) to penetrate even one inch inside the body. Over time, however, you want to be able to progressively feel every cubic inch of space inside your body. (pg. 86)

After practicing this mind-only technique, many delude themselves, certain that they can feel their insides when in fact they cannot. It may help to remember that once you can feel the inside of your body clearly, with some effort you should be able to move any given part of your internal body at will, no matter how slightly. You could simply have someone with sensitive hands give you a reality check as to whether or not your perceptions of your abilities correspond to what is actually happening. (pg. 86)

It is important to actually feel your body and not to merely visualize its different parts. This process of internally sensing the body starting at the head and moving down to the lower tantien can take a long time; indeed, you can spend a one-hour session of meditation working on only a small segment of your body. After gaining experience, your ability to feel inside and penetrate your body with awareness will intensify. At this point you should be gaining the ability to actually feel your internal sensations. As you move your attention through your body, you will probably encounter areas that feel full of all sorts of internal content-things stuck, blocked, uncomfortable, agitated, happy, depressed, and so on. These and all other Taoist meditation practices ultimately involve dissolving and releasing the energy of these blockages, as described in the next chapter, until you become internally free. (pg. 88)

Appendix C

American-Chinese Cross-Cultural Analysis of Round

In this section, we will look at both the American and Chinese conceptual understandings of the word round or circular. As you will see, the concept of round or circular has different meanings in our two cultures. Developing an appreciation of these differences may help you bridge the culture-gap in this aspect of your training. It may also help you understand what you are trying to accomplish in "rounding the crotch" from a cultural point of view.

In both Chinese language and American English, the word round or circular is used to describe objects of that shape. This section focuses on the other culturally embedded meanings. It is in this area that we find significant differences in the meaning of round and circular. And it is in these differences that confusion arises.

The book "Beyond Culture" (published 1976) by the American anthropologist Edward T. Hall (1914-2009), includes what he defined as low-context and high-context cultures.

> A high-context (HC) communication or message is one in which most of the information is either in the physical context or internalized in the person, while very little is in the coded, explicit, transmitted part of the message. A low-context (LC) communication is just the opposite, i.e., the mass of the information is vested in the explicit code. (pg. 79)

> Although no culture exists exclusively at one end of the scale, some are high while others are low. American culture, while not on

the bottom, is toward the lower end of the scale. We are still considerably above the German-Swiss, the Germans, and the Scandinavians in the amount of contexting needed in everyday life. …. China, the possessor of a great and complex culture, is on the high-context end of the scale. (pg. 79)

So when we consider the word round or circle, in a low-context culture like the U.S., the more colloquial usages of the word carries less information in comparison to a high-context culture like China where colloquial usages of the word carries more information. Specific examples of this will be seen in the next two sections. Let's begin with building a foundation on the more familiar American understanding.

American Understanding of Round

In American English, the word round carries many meanings. The list below is likely neither exhaustive nor inclusive of all the local colloquial and slang expressions that you may have heard or used. However, if you are an American-English speaker, reading this list should give you a reasonable insight into the variety of meanings we apply to the words round and circle.

- A round - each of a succession of stages. A set in a sequence. One shot of ammunition.
- A round of applause - a show of audience approval
- Sing a round - a song where each singer sings the same theme but start one after another
- Making or going on rounds - walking a particular route.
- Round up - a gathering together.
- Talking/walking in circles - lacking clarity. Unable to get to a destination. Confused.
- A round trip - to travel to a destination and return to the point you started from.

Appendix C: American-Chinese Cross-Cultural Analysis of Round

- Going round and round - follow a circular course. Repeat the same argument and never reach a conclusion.
- Round-about - not direct, not efficient.
- Year round - something happens without ceasing for an entire year.
- Round out - to fill in a gap, supplement a lack, make more complete.
- Round off - to make the edges or corners of something smoother.
- A round number - to increase or decrease a number to a preferred unit.

From the examples in the list above, we see that the word round and circle expresses concepts related to: sets, walking an established route, inefficiency or confusion, time measurement, supplementing lack/completing wholeness, returning from whence you started. And so if these phrases and concepts formed your conceptual reality, how then would you apply these to understand the instruction to "round the crotch"? Suddenly we are confronted with the possibility that the Chinese understanding of round and circular may be something completely different.

Chinese Understanding of Round

As an American, I naturally apply my linguistic and cultural understanding of *round* in my attempt to understand the Chinese cultural and linguistic meaning of *round*. And this is where communication breaks down. (Obviously, if your native language and culture is not English-speaking American, you would want to explore the varied meanings of the word *round* and *circular* in your native language and culture using the model I've employed here.)

Various authors describe the ancient Chinese models of the universe; the ancient Chinese cosmology as the heaven being round and the earth being square. Given the understanding that humans represent a microcosm of the macrocosm, roundness has a special meaning in Chinese culture. Let's look at a few examples.

Maxine Hong Kingston, in her book "The Woman Warrior: Memoirs of a Girlhood Among Ghosts" tells a story from her childhood in China of an aunt who became pregnant long after her husband went to America. Here's an excerpt from Chapter 1 titled, "No Name Woman":

> The round moon cakes and round doorways, the round tables of graduated sizes that fit one roundness inside another, round windows and rice bowls – these talismans had lost their power to warn this family of the law; a family must be whole, faithfully keeping the descent line by having sons to feed the old and the dead, who in turn look after the family. The villagers came to show my aunt and her lover-in-hiding a broken house. The villagers were speeding up the circling of events because she was too short-sighted to see that her infidelity had already harmed the village, that waves of consequences would return unpredictably, as now, to hurt her. This roundness had to be made coin-sized so that she would see its circumference: punish her at the birth of her baby. (pg. 13)

In "No Name Woman" we see that circular or round objects serve as talismans. Roundness infers that the social order is functioning properly. There is completeness. There is harmony. There are no breaks. Roundness infers integration. Roundness values the whole over the individual part or member. The group's survival depends on the individual members working together as one. When the roundness is broken, that's when trouble arises.

For a wonderful analysis of the Chinese meaning of round, Here are several quotes from the book: "Understanding Global Cultures: Metaphorical Journeys Through 31 Nations, Clusters of Nations, Continents, and Diversity", Fifth Edition (2012) by Martin J. Gannon and Rajnandini (Raj) K. Pillai. These quotes are all from Chapter 26 "The Chinese Family Altar" (pg. 448-460).

Appendix C: American-Chinese Cross-Cultural Analysis of Round

---

Chinese society is neither individualistic nor collectivistic as are other family-based ethnic groups; instead, it is based on relations (Bond, 1986). Confucians, for example, feel that individuals have roles they must fulfill but that, in doing so, their individualism can enlarge and enrich them for the greater good of the family and kinship group. From the Chinese perspective, people exist only in relation to others (Chen, 2001). (pg. 449)

The specific aspects of the altar are roundness, symbolizing the continuity and structural completeness of the family; representation of harmony within the family and the broader society; and fluidity or the capacity to change while maintaining solid traditions. (pg. 450)

In short, expatriate Chinese are similar to traditional Chinese in the sense that the family is the basic social unit through which all are united in a relation-based system. Roundness is emphasized by these families, who form a complex but informal network throughout the world, as are harmony and fluidity. (pg. 452)

Roundness, the first of the three characteristics of the family altar, stands for the continuity and structural completeness of the family. It symbolizes that the family is the basic, distinct, and enduring feature of the Chinese culture. ... All of the efforts of the living are directed toward obtaining a rounded family in which the descent line is preserved. Thus roundness suggests a unity of the family circle that is related to the structural ideal of flawless Chinese patriarchy. Male children (especially the oldest son), who are obligated to perform ceremonial and ancestral rites, are preferred over female children. Hence roundness also suggests that men should have wives who can bear sons. (pg. 454)

This rounded conception of familial relationships is distinctively Chinese, and it encompasses members of the family over space and time. The family, rather than the individual, has been the basic unit of social organization among the Chinese since the time of the Duke of Chou in the 12th century BCE. (pg. 456)

Furthermore, the concept of roundness helps to explain the well-known Chinese practice of guanxi. As indicated in the previous chapter, from the Chinese perspective, a person exists only in relation to others. (pg. 456)

Roundness is a necessary but not sufficient condition for the second characteristic of the family altar, harmony. The ideally harmonious family is one in which there are few if any quarrels, financial problems, or illnesses. (pg. 458)

The major sense of security and harmony comes from the rounded family and the all-encompassing family altar. (pg. 458)

The third characteristic of the family altar is fluidity or the capacity to change while maintaining solid traditions. It reflects the relation-oriented approach of the Chinese" (pg. 458)

In summary, we see that *round* carries in conjunction with harmony and fluidity, the connotation of integration and an all-encompassing connection. Roundness identifies who is in the circle and who is out. Unity. Continuity and structural completeness. Relationship. You either have *round* or you don't. This notion of roundness permeates Chinese culture. Let's now turn to how this notion or concept of round shows up in the Chinese language.

Further investigation into this cultural meaning of *round*, can be found in online dictionary searches for the Chinese word for round which is (圆; yuán). We see that *round* can refer to anything round, circular, or spherical, however, depending on the context in which (圆; yuán) appears, *round* may also contribute to other meanings. For example, consider how *round* (圆; yuán) is used in combination with other words:

(团圆; tuán yuán) to have a family reunion

Appendix C: American-Chinese Cross-Cultural Analysis of Round

(圆月 ; yuán yuè) full moon

(圆满 ; yuán mǎn) complete or satisfactory

(圆寂 ; yuán jì) for Buddhist nuns and priests means "completing the peace"; to pass away; to die

(圆场 ; yuán chǎng) to mediate; to help effect a compromise

(圆房; yuán fang) to consummate marriage

(圆梦; yuán mèng) to interpret dreams

(圆滑; yuán huá) tactful, shrewd, smooth

(圆软; yuán ruǎn) round-soft; pliable (desired quality of body in qigong)

(圆润; yuán rùn) plump-moist, mellow; full; mature, fluent technique

(圆谎; yuán huǎng) to straighten out contradictions in a lie and make it plausible

(自圆其说; zì yuán qí shuō) make one's statement consistent; justify oneself

(汤圆; tāngyuán) the small, sweet glutenous rice balls served on the last day of the Chinese New Year celebration, a holiday in which families reunite.

In addition to individual words, here are several phrases and proverbs in Chinese which serve as examples of how the word *round* is used. This may help you further appreciate the breadth of how *round* is embedded in Chinese culture.

Here are a few Chinese proverbs from "A Collection of Chinese Proverbs, by William Scarborough" (1875). In order of appearance, #99, #830, #1462. I've substituted both the old style Chinese characters with simplified characters and substituted the pre-Wade-Giles Romanization with Pin-yin.

砍 的 没 得 车 的 圆 (kǎn de méi de chē de yuán)
"What is chopped has not the roundness of what is turned." (#99)
My Understanding: To achieve proper functioning takes time.

明 月 不 常 圜, 彩 雲 容 易 散 (míng yuè bù cháng yuán, cǎi yún róng yì sàn)
"The bright moon is not round for long, the brilliant cloud is easily scattered." (#830)
My understanding: Fullness and harmony can easily be broken.

转弯摸角,处处合得若 (zhuǎn wān mō jiǎo, chù chù hé ruò)
"Who rub off corners and round curves wind, will everywhere peace and concord find." (#1462)
My understanding: If you don't want to offend someone, then don't say something directly. Consider the implications on everyone involved before speaking or acting.

The article, *More Than Just A Circle And Square: Shapes In Chinese Culture* by Kane Guo (April 23, 2012) is worth a read. Here are a couple quotes from that article found at the illuminantpartners.com site:

Chinese: 他可算是圆了当年的梦想 (tā kě suàn shì yuán lè dāng nián de mèng xiǎng)
English: He's finally made his lifelong dream a reality.
Meaning: "圆" ([pinyin] yuán, circle, is used as a verb, meaning "to fulfill", "to perfect".

Chinese: 现在你可算是功德圆满了 (xiàn zài nǐ kě suàn shì gōng dé yuán mǎn le)
English: Now you can say that you've achieved all goals.

Meaning: "圆满" (yuán mǎn), round and full, means "the ultimate completeness".

And here a couple more phrases one of my Chinese friends told me:

Chinese: 美国人的头是方的;中国人的头是圆的

English: American head is square. Chinese head is round.
Meaning: Americans get right to the point; tend to be blunt and say what's on their mind. Chinese talk around the point, tend to conceal their real feeling, tend to consider the effect on everyone involved before speaking.

Chinese: 你想画圆; 但是你画得不圆

English: You want to draw the circle but you can't draw a good circle.
Meaning: You want to make good relations but you're not skillful to do so. You're a bad liar.

In summary, as you've seen, in Chinese culture, round (圆) carries much broader and deeper meaning than its American English counterpart. In terms of internal martial art practice, I understand that "rounding the crotch" can be interpreted from its deeper cultural meaning of developing connection between the bottom, middle, and top of the body, making it whole. An "A" shaped or pointed crotch is one which breaks the connection between the bottom and top. Since power resides in the unbroken whole, a break at the crotch cuts off the power of the legs to the upper body. Hence, this is why it is important to "round the crotch".

Appendix D

Historical Use of Medical Rectal Dilators

There is a twofold purpose in presenting this review of rectal dilation that has appeared in the medical literature. First is to demonstrate that the use of rectal dilators has been documented as a medical therapy for more than 100 years. Second, is to provide this "clinical" perspective to those who may only be familiar with the slang term "butt plug" as a device to be used for auto-erogenous or anal sexual activity. My hope is that this information will provide you with a reasonable perspective on this device. As with any aspect of internal martial art training, let your purpose and intention guide you.

A Broad Historical Overview

<u>American Journal of Gastroenterology</u> Robert Kravetz MD, MACG, Chairman, Archives Committee, American College of Gastroenterology. "Rectal Dilators", v.96, no.9. (September 2001).

> Rectal diseases have plagued mankind for millennia. The earliest mention of them is found in the Code of Hammurabi, about 2200 BC. Instructions to the patient state "pay the doctor five shekels for curing a diseased bowel." The famous Egyptian "Ebers Papyrus," about 1500 BC, mentions hemorrhoids. Hippocrates, 400 BC, used a rectal speculum. For the next 1500 years, rectal diseases, hemorrhoids, fistulae, prolapse, etc were treated with cautery, ligatures, and caustics.

Aside from rectal strictures related to disease, these therapies resulted in additional strictures. Many were treated with a variety of rectal dilators, which was preferable to surgical intervention. Various forms of instrumentation were used. It is surprising to note that the opening of a stricture, although extremely small, could maintain adequate bowel function.

Graded dilators of various sizes have been used for the past 100 years with great success. This set of Dr. Young's Improved Rectal Dilators was sold by prescription in drugstores for $3.75 in the 1920s. They are no different from current dilators and would be equally effective today.

1896
Homœopathic Journal of Obstetrics, Gynecology and Pedology, Edited by B.F. Underwood, M.D. Vol.18, No.5, New York 1896. "Uterine Atrophy" by Eugene Hubbell, M.D. pg 487-491

Case IV. Mrs. C., aet. Forty-eight. Passed climacteric four years ago, since which time she has been feeling ill, saying she was going to die, or that she was dying; weak heart action, palpitation, dyspepsia, pain in the back and left side under shoulder; constipated bowels move only after cathartics or injections; very despondent; frequent deep sighing respirations. Uterus atrophied, retroverted, pale, non-sensitive. Treatment: passed sounds once in two weeks (four times in all) up to Nos. 12 and 14, English scale. Applied clycoid; also had her use a rectal dilator twice a week. Improvement from the first, till in a few weeks all symptoms had disappeared, except pain or ache by self-suggestions (or Christian Science?). She formerly had no appetite, and was very pale and anaemic, but now all is changed. She is bright and cheerful, attends to her own household duties, and says nothing about dying.

Appendix D: Historical Use of Medical Rectal Dilators

1898

<u>Advertisement for Dr. Weirick's Improved Self-Retaining Rectal Dilators</u>. Canadian Journal of Medicine and Surgery, Vol 3, No 6, June, 1898. pg xliv.

> For the cure of Piles, Constipation, Rheumatism, Insomnia, Dyspepsia and all chronic diseases caused by a faulty condition of the circulation. Their use relaxes the sphincters, stimulates the sympathetic nervous system, equalizes the circulation, relieving congestion and in this way effects a cure.

1910

<u>Texas State Journal of Medicine, Society News. Vol. 5</u>, No.7. Texas Medical Association. November 1909. pg. 291.

> Dr. John T. Moore said the one method of cure not mentioned is the cure by rectal dilators. In Galveston the druggists are curing piles right along. Every case of piles is not an operative case. Pile operations are rather serious ones, and may result in the death of the patient. Dr. Keiller, of Galveston, worked out a method anatomically that theoretically ought to be all right. His plan was to dissect up the mucous membrane and remove the veins, and then suture the membrane back in place. In people leading inactive, sedentary lives piles could often be cured by a course in a gymnasium. There are quite a number of cases cured by simple dilatation.

1915

<u>Stricture of the Rectum</u>. Texas State Journal of Medicine. Volume 11.No.8. December 1915. By Venable, C. pg. 441-442.

> In four of my cases infection supervened, and while draining I inserted a long conical metal rectal dilator, which was worn in the rectum and only removed for stool or flatus. This the patients could

do themselves without discomfort. This prevented constricting bands of scar tissue forming in the infected peri-rectal area.

1920
Journal of the American Medical Association. Volume 75, Issues 1-13, (1920). pg. 565. Regarding a patient history...

> He had no constipation, yet he said the stool was very small. At a variable time after eating this distress would come on and he would have to use an enema to obtain relief. For some time past he had been using rectal dilators nearly every morning, and thought they were a great help. His trouble was attributed to his work, i.e., lifting and carrying heavy articles.

circa 1925
A historical picture of Young's Rectal Dilator, ca1925 from the Historical Research Center Digital Collections:
http://hrcdigitalcoll.uams.edu/cdm/singleitem/collection/uw/id/682/rec/1

1940s
Inner Hygiene: Constipation and the Pursuit of Health in Modern Society. by James C. Whorton, pg. 245.

> in the 1940s, "Non-drug methods were also promoted by naturopathy. *Nature's Path* brimmed with ads for enema equipment and rectal dilators..."

1947
Rectal Dilator in Perineal Repair. Hudgins A.P. West Virginia Medical Journal. 1947 Nov;43(11):370.

Appendix D: Historical Use of Medical Rectal Dilators

1948

Rectal Dilators in the Treatment of Constipation. Finkel MD, Levine AJ. Journal Lancet. 1948 Dec;68(12):467.

Spasm and Fibrosis of the Sphincter and Due to Reflex Action. By Francis.C. Newton, M.D. and Charles A. MacGregor, M.D. New England Journal of Medicine. 1948 July; v.239, no.4. pg:113-116.

> If no abnormality other than spasm is found, a high-residue diet without catharsis may be resumed immediately. Beginning on the fourth day in the uncomplicated case, rectal dilation should be performed daily, either digitally or by the use of Young's dilators (Fig. 5). These consist of a series of graduated dilators, which may be passed by the patient with the aid of a small amount of lubricating jelly, beginning with the smallest and working up to the largest size each time. The daily dilation should be continued as long as is required to re-establish normal bowel habits. Periodic rectal examinations should be made by the physician to detect any tendency to recurrence of the anal spasm.

1950

The Treatment of Constipation, with Reference to the Use of Rectal Dilators. by Hudgins, A.P., American Practitioner and Digest of Treatment, [1950, 1(12):1260-1262]

1973

Dilator for Treatment of Strictures in the Upper Part of the Rectum and the Sigmoid. Dencker H, Johansson JI, Norryd C, Tranberg KG. Diseases of the Colon and Rectum. 1973 Nov-Dec;16(6):550-2

2002

Handbook of Pharmacy Health Care: Diseases and Patient Advice (2nd ed), by Robin J. Harman, Pamela Mason. Pharmaceutical Press, September 2002, Medical - 604 pages. pg 30, 1.8 "Anorectal disorders"

> Adoption of a high-fibre diet (e.g. bran), administration of faecal softeners (BNF 1.6.3) and application of topical soothing agents (BNF 1.7.1) are all beneficial and are used in conjunction with rectal dilators. Bathing in warm salt water may also provide relief. Surgery may be necessary for chronic fissures.

2003

Journal of Pediatric Gastroenterology and Nutrition 36:403–406 © March 2003 Lippincott Williams & Wilkins, Inc., Philadelphia "Case Report: Anorectal Strictures and Genital Crohn Disease: An Unusual Clinical Association" *Omar I. Saadah, *Mark R. Oliver, *Julie E. Bines, †Keith B. Stokes, and *Donald J. S. Cameron

> Anorectal stricture was present when diagnosis was made in four patients; the others developed strictures within the subsequent 4.5 years despite ongoing maximal medical therapy. Strictures were first detected by digital examination in the office and subsequently assessed by examination during anesthesia. In most patients, the strictures were sufficiently tight to prevent the full insertion of the examining finger or the colonoscope. The characteristics of the strictures are described in Table 2.

> Severe strictures were defined as those which were tight (limiting digital examination and insertion of a colonoscope), friable with easy bleeding during dilatation, and requiring repeated dilatation in addition to maximum medical therapy. All dilatations were performed by one surgeon (K.B.S.) using rectal dilators up to sizes 17 to 23, depending on severity.

Appendix D: Historical Use of Medical Rectal Dilators

2012
Pamela Morrison Physical Therapy, P.C.
http://www.pamelamorrisonpt.com
(Selected for the 2009, 2010, 2011 and 2012 New York Award in the Physical Therapists.)

Anismus, also known as pelvic floor hypertonicity, anal sphincter dysserynergia, dyssynergic defecation, and paradoxal puborectalis dysfunction, is a disorder of the external anal sphincter and puborectalis muscles (one of the pelvic floor muscles) upon attempted bowel movement. It is a form of pelvic floor muscle dysfunction. …

One of the expert pelvic therapists at Pamela Morrison Physical Therapy will perform a complete history and physical exam. Close inspection of your pelvic alignment and pelvic floor muscles and sphincter will occur. Pelvic nerve tests will also occur. … The manual therapies and modalities such as electrical stimulation help to eliminate the muscle pain and spasm. The use of rectal dilator therapy may also prove beneficial.

Appendix E

Chinese Martial Arts Magazines in China

Official Website of Wenxian Wushu Association
http://www.cntjq.net/

China Taijiquan Magazine (中国太极拳)
http://www.zcom.com/m/zhongguotaijiquan/

Jingwu Magazine (精武)
http://wuxizazhi.cnki.net/Magazine/JWZZ201101.html

Wudang Magazine (武当)
http://wuxizazhi.cnki.net/Magazine/WDZZ201202.html

Shaolin and Taiji Magazine (少林与太极)
http://wuxizazhi.cnki.net/Magazine/SLTA201210.html
http://www.cqvip.com/QK/81942X/

For Chen style research papers, see the Xiamen Taiji site:
http://www.xmtaiji.net/

References

This list is excessive for a book this size. Because I don't have any professional training in Kinesiology, Sports Medicine, Physical Therapy, Massage, etc., and only my practical experience, I really didn't know which sources were authoritative in their field. I looked for anything to inform and support my purpose. I learned as I read. Some materials overlap and some have unique perspectives. In the end, these are the sources I referenced for the data element of this book. Some sources will be more accessible to some readers than others.

Advertisement for Dr. Weirick's Improved Self-Retaining Rectal Dilators. (1898). *Canadian Journal of Medicine and Surgery, Vol 3, No 6, June, pg xliv.*

Alva, M. (2012, May 30). De stress with pelvic floor awareness exercise part 1 [Video File]. Retrieved from http://www.youtube.com/watch?v=_jWCCLG46js

Asher, Anne. (2009, August 23). Pelvic floor strengthening: pelvic floor contraction and a word of caution about doing pelvic floor exercise. Retrieved from http://backandneck.about.com/od/pelvicfloor/ss/pelvicfloorstre_2.htm

Asher, Anne. (2009, August 23). Pelvic floor strengthening: tips and considerations. Retrieved from http://backandneck.about.com/od/pelvicfloor/ss/pelvicfloorstre_7.htm

Asher, A. (2009, August 23). Find the inward squeeze. Retrieved from http://backandneck.about.com/od/pelvicfloor/ss/pelvicfloorstre_3.htm

Asher, A. (2009, August 23). Determine strength and endurance of your pelvic floor contractions. Retrieved from http://backandneck.about.com/od/pelvicfloor/ss/pelvicfloorstre_4.htm

Austin, P. (2001). Bio mechanics of pelvis and low back pain: introduction to pelvic and hip biomechanics. http://www.scribd.com/doc/23822321/PDF-Bio-Mechanics-of-Pelvis-Pelvis-and-Low-Back-Pain

Avni, O. The story down under - the pelvic floor muscles. Retrieved February 26, 2013 from

http://www.selfgrowth.com/articles/the_story_down_under.html

Barsotti, A. Ode to the pelvic floor. Retrieved February 26, 2013 from http://pilatesunion.com/news/34/

Betsch, M., Schneppendahl, J., Dor, L., Jungbluth, P., Grassmann, Jan. (2011). Influence of foot positions on the spine and pelvis. *Arthritis Care & Research, Vol. 63, No. 12, December 2011, pp 1758–1765.*

Bingham, A. (2012, November 3). What happens in the pelvis, doesn't stay in the pelvis. Message posted to http://transformationzoneyoga.com/2012/11/03/what-happens-in-the-pelvis-doesnt-stay-in-the-pelvis/

Bluhm, D. (2005). Elements of well-organized action. http://www.siskiyouaikikai.org/elements.well.pdf

Bo, K. & Berghmans, B. & Morkved, S. & Van Kampen, M. (2007). Evidence-based physical therapy for the pelvic floor: bridging science and clinical practice. Churchill Livingstone.

Bowman, K. (2010, June 10). Pelvic floor demystified [Video File]. Retrieved from http://www.youtube.com/watch?v=IOoTC9DpB3k

Bowman, K. (2012, April 25). A too tight pelvic floor. Message posted to http://www.alignedandwell.com/katysays/atootightpelvicfloor/

Bowman, K. (2012, April 30). Too tight pelvic floor 2. Message posted to http://www.alignedandwell.com/katysays/tootightpelvicfloor-2/

Bowman, K. (2012, December 17). Neutral pelvis 2. Message posted to http://www.alignedandwell.com/katysays/neutral-pelvis-2/

Bowman, K. (2012, August 31). Ramblings from my pelvis. Message posted to http://www.alignedandwell.com/katysays/ramblings-from-my-pelvis/

Bowman, K. (2010, June 2). You don't know squat. Retrieved from http://www.alignedandwell.com/katysays/you-dont-know-squat/

References

Bowman, K. (2012, August 22). Men have pelves too. Message posted to http://www.alignedandwell.com/katysays/men-have-pelves-too/

Bowman, K. (2011, August 29). High heels, pelvic floor and bad science. Message posted to http://www.alignedandwell.com/katysays/high-heels-pelvic-floor-and-bad-science/

Bowman, K. (2010, July 6). Mind your pelvis. Message posted to http://www.alignedandwell.com/katysays/mind-your-pelvis/

Bowman, K. (2010, June 22). What a waist. Message posted to http://www.alignedandwell.com/katysays/what-a-waist/

Bowman, K. (2010, May 7). 1,2,3,4 we like our pelvic floor. Message posted to http://www.alignedandwell.com/katysays/1234-we-like-our-pelvic-floor/

Bowman, K. (2010, May 7). Have psoas will travel. Message posted to http://www.alignedandwell.com/katysays/have-psoas-will-travel/

Bowman, K. (2010, April 28). Low hanging fruit. Message posted to http://www.alignedandwell.com/katysays/low-hanging-fruit/

Bridge building shared knowledge commons. Retrieved Feb 26, 2013 from http://physicsofoz.pbworks.com/w/page/24731138/Shared%20Knowledge

Bridges (How arches work). Retrieved Feb 26, 2013 from http://www.bristol.ac.uk/civilengineering/bridges/Pages/HowtoreadabridgeArches.html

Brook, M. (June, 2009). The importance of scar tissue release therapy. *Massage Today, Vol. 09, Issue 06*.Caile, C. A simple lesson in body mechanics. Retrieved Feb 26, 2013 from http://www.fightingarts.com/reading/article.php?id=28

Calais-Germain, B. (2006). Anatomy of breathing. Seattle, WA: Eastland Press.

Carriere, B. & Markel Feldt, C. (2006). The pelvic floor. Stuttgart, Germany. Georg Thiem Verlag.

Chaitow, L. & Lovegrove Jones, R. (2012). Chronic pelvic pain and dysfunction: practical physical medicine, 1st edition. Chapter 2.2: Anatomy and biomechanics of the pelvis.

Chaitow, L. (2006, December). The pelvic floor paradox. *Massage Today, Vol 6, Issue 12.*
http://www.massagetoday.com/mpacms/mt/article.php?id=13515

Chang, S. (1986). The complete system of self-healing internal exercises. Reno, NV: Tao Publishing.

Chen Village. What are the body requirements of tai chi? Message posted to http://www.chenvillage.com/what-are-the-body-requirements-of-tai-chi

Chen, X. 陈鑫 (2007). The illustrated canon of chen family taijiquan (太极拳图说陈式). English version translated by Alex Golstein, 2007. Australia: INBI Matrix Pty Ltd.

Cohen, K. (1999). The way of qigong: the art and science of chinese energy healing. Random House Publishing.

Continence Foundation of Australia. 10 step guide to pelvic floor safe exercise. Retrieved February 26, 2013 from
http://www.pelvicfloorfirst.org.au/pages/how-can-i-make-my-program-pelvic-floor-safe.html

Crawford, N. Stop doing kegels: real pelvic floor advice for women (and men). Retrieved Feb 16, 2013 from
http://breakingmuscle.com/womens-fitness/stop-doing-kegels-real-pelvic-floor-advice-women-and-men

D'Arezo, P. (2003). Posture alignment: the missing link in health and fitness. Colorado Springs, CO: Marcellina MountainPress.

Daniel, V. (2008, October 5). Wilhelm Reich and His Influence. Retrieved from
http://www.sonoma.edu/users/d/daniels/reichlecture.html

Dencker, H., Johansson, J., Norryd, C., & Tranberg, K. (1973). Dilator for treatment of strictures in the upper part of the rectum and the sigmoid. *Diseases of the Colon and Rectum, Nov-Dec;16(6):550-2*

Diepersloot, Jan. (1995). Warriors of stillness vol. I: meditative traditions in the chinese martial arts. Walnut Creek, CA: Center for the Healing Arts.

References

Dobias, D. (2010, June 2). Hip and lower back pain exercises [Video File]. Retrieved from http://www.youtube.com/watch?v=WcOPgXRo4Yg

Editor. (2006, July 20). Function and usage of the kua: q & a with chen zhonghua. Message posted to http://internalartsia.wordpress.com/2006/07/20/function-and-usage-of-the-kua/

Editor. (2005). Perineal massage in pregnancy. *The Journal of Midwifery and Women's Health*. *Vol 50, No 1, January/February*, pg 63-64. Retrieved from http://www.midwife.org/Share-With-Women

Ellis-Christensen, T. (2010, November 14). What is a muscle spasm? Message posted to http://www.wisegeek.com/what-is-a-muscle-spasm.htm#slideshow

Fain, M. (2012, June 23). The alignment issue. Are your back and hips really out of alignment? Message posted to http://spokanephysicaltherapist.wordpress.com/2012/06/23/the-alignment-issue-are-your-back-and-hips-really-out-of-alignment/

Felice, J. (2009, September 9). Can connective tissue store emotional patterns. Message posted to http://connectivetissue.wordpress.com/2009/09/09/can-our-connective-tissue-store-emotional-patterns/

Findley, T. (2011, January 15). Fascia - architecture of connective tissue [Video File]. Dr. Tom Findley summarizes a 1988 Ph.D. thesis, The Architecture of Connective Tissue in the Musculoskeletal System by Japp Van der Wal, M.D., Ph.D. Retrieved from http://www.youtube.com/watch?v=rGzM6rpS4j8

Finkel, M. & Levine, A. (1948). Rectal dilators in the treatment of constipation. *Journal Lancet, Dec;68(12):467*.

Fogel, A. (2012, April 19) Emotional and physical pain activate similar brain regions. Retrieved from http://www.psychologytoday.com/blog/body-sense/201204/emotional-and-physical-pain-activate-similar-brain-regions

Franklin, E. (2003). Pelvic power: mind/body exercises for strength, flexibility, posture, and balance for men and women. Highstown, NJ: Elysian Editions, Princeton Book Company.

Frantzis, B. (2010). Dragon and tiger medical qigong, volume 1: Develop health and energy in 7 simple movements. North Atlantic Books.

Frantzis, B. (2005). <u>Opening the energy gates of your body: Qigong for lifelong health.</u> Berkeley, CA: <u>Blue Snake Books.</u>

Frantzis, B. (2001). The great stillness: The water method of taoist meditation series, vol. 2. Fairfax, CA: Energy Arts.

Ganon, M. & Pillai, R. (2012). Understanding global cultures: metaphorical journeys through 31 nations, clusters of nations, continents, and diversity, Fifth Edition. Chapter 26 "The Chinese Family Altar" (pgs. 448-460). Thousand Oaks, CA: SAGE Publications.

Ge, J. (2002, September). Small frame of chen style taijiquan. Message posted to <u>http://www.chinafrominside.com/ma/taiji/xiaojia.html</u>

Geraci, M., & Brown, W. (2005). Evidence-based treatment of hip and pelvic injuries in runners. *Phys Med Rehabil Clin N Am 16*, 711–747.

Giammatteo, S. (2003). Integrative manual therapy for biomechanics application of muscle energy and & beyond technique. Integrated Manual Therapy Series: Volume 3. Berkeley, CA: North Atlantic Books.

Gibson, J. Male Pelvic Floor: Advanced Bodywork and Massage. <u>http://www.malepelvicfloor.com/</u>

Gibson, J. (2010). The pelvic floor. Message posted to <u>http://coremassage4men.com/index.html</u>

Guo, K. (2012, April 23). More than just a circle and square: shapes in chinese culture. Message posted to <u>http://www.illuminantpartners.com/2012/04/23/more-than-just-a-circle-and-squareshapes-chinese-culture/</u>

Harman, R. & Mason, P. (2002). 1.8 Anorectal disorders. In *Handbook of Pharmacy Health Care: Diseases and Patient Advice (2nd ed)* pg 30. London, UK: Pharmaceutical Press.

Hedley, G. (2009, February 7). The fuzz speech [Video File]. Retrieved from <u>http://www.youtube.com/watch?v=_FtSP-tkSug</u>

Hedley, G. (2012, April 7). Reconsidering "the fuzz" Part 2 [Video File]. Retrieved from <u>http://www.youtube.com/watch?v=D0LlR7Bq0So</u>

References

Hedley, G. (2013, January 26). Integral anatomy series [Video File]. Retrieved from http://www.youtube.com/watch?v=K68kC9R7THc

Hodges, P. & Sapsford, R. & Pengel, L. (2007). Postural and respiratory functions of the pelvic floor muscles. *Neurourology and Urodynamics 26:362–371.*

Holstege, G., Bandler, R., & Saper, C. (1996). The emotional motor system. Amsterdam: Elsevier Science.

Hopkinson, C. (2012). Biomechanics - How your body moves. http://www.experiencewellness.co.uk/media/Information%20sheets/i%20move%20freely%20article.pdf

Hubbell, E. (1896). Uterine atrophy. In Underwood, B. (Ed.), *Homœopathic Journal of Obstetrics, Gynecology and Pedology*, Vol.18, No.5 (pp 487-491). New York. A.I. Chatterton & Co.

Hudgins, A. (1947). Rectal dilator in perineal repair. *West Virginia Medical Journal, Nov;43(11):370.*

Hudgins, A. (1950). The treatment of constipation, with reference to the use of rectal dilators. *American Practitioner and Digest of Treatment, 1(12):1260-1262.*

First International Fascia Research Congress. (2007). http://www.fasciacongress.org/2007/

Second International Fascia Research Congress. (2009). http://www.fasciacongress.org/2009/

Third International Fascia Research Congress (2012). http://www.fasciacongress.org/2012/

Ironside, S. Who cares about pelvic alignment? Retrieved February 26, 2013 from http://www.ultrafitness.net/pelvic%20alignment.pdf

Isacowitz, R & Clippinger, K. Core stability plays key role in body alignment. Message posted to
http://www.humankinetics.com/excerpts/excerpts/core-stability-plays-key-role-in-body-alignment

Janda, S. (2006, January 30). Biomechanics of the pelvic floor musculature. Ph.D. Dissertation for Technical University of Delft, Netherlands.

http://repository.tudelft.nl/view/ir/uuid%3A68ded298-7765-4490-9c7f-1d079a9a9c7e/

Jou, T. (1980). The dao of tai-chi chuan: way to rejuvenation. Piscataway, NJ: Tai Chi Foundation.

Kirchhoff, T. The internal athletics. Retrieved February 26, 2013 from http://www.futaichi.com/IntAth.html

Knights, K. What is the perineal nerve? Retrieved February 26, 2013 from http://www.wisegeek.com/what-is-the-perineal-nerve.htm#

Kohn, L. (2008). Chinese healing exercises: The tradition of daoyin. 1st edition. University of Hawaii Press.

Kravetz, R. (2001). Rectal dilators. *American Journal of Gastroenterology*, v.96, no.9. pg 2768.

KungfuMagazine.com (2012, January). Message posted to http://ezine.kungfumagazine.com/forum/showthread.php?t=62944

Kurtz, R. & Prestera, H. (1984). The body reveals: What your body says about you. New York N.Y.: HarperCollins Publishers.

Lam, T. (2003, September 3). How to align your body for better qi flow: A guide to the correct practice of taijiquan. Message posted to http://tukylam.freeoda.com/practiceguide.html

Lam, T. (2003, September 3). On stance, kua (hips) and dang (crotch). Message posted to http://tukylam.freeoda.com/egroup4.html

Lee, D. (2004). The pelvic girdle: an approach to the examination and treatment of the lumbopelvic-hip region. 3rd edition. London: Churchill Livingstone.

Lee, D. (2005). Pelvic stability & your core. Presented in whole or part at the: American Back Society Meeting – San Francisco 2005, BC Trial Lawyers Meeting – Vancouver 2005, Japanese Society of Posture & Movement Meeting – Tokyo 2006.
http://dianelee.ca/articles/2PelvicStability&Yourcore.pdf

Lee, D. (2010). The pelvic girdle: An integration of clinical expertise and research. 4th edition.

Lee, D. Training for the deep muscles of the core. Retrieved February 26, 2013 from http://dianelee.ca/education/article_deep_core.php

Lee, D. Pelvic floor muscles. Retrieved February 26, 2013 from http://dianelee.ca/articles/PELVICFLOOR.pdf

References

Left Wing Taoist. (2011, November 14). Finding and activating pelvis floor muscles. Message posted to http://internalkungfuireland.blogspot.com/2011/11/finding-and-activating-pelvis-floor.html

Levine, C. (2011, April 19). Pelvic floor health - strengthening your core. Message posted to http://www.womentowomen.com/urinaryincontinence/pelvicfloorhealth.aspx

Lo, B. (1979). The essence of t'ai chi ch'uan: the literary tradition. Richmond, CA: North Atlantic Books.

Loughray, A. (2006, July 27). Cycling, wedges and biomechanics. http://www.ezilon.com/articles/articles/2270/1/Cycling,-wedges-and-biomechanics

Lowen, A. (1994). Bioenergetics: the revolutionary therapy that uses the language of the body to heal the problems of the mind. Arkana.

Lowen, A. (1996). Joy. Arkana.

Lowen, A. & Lowen, L. (2003). Way to vibrant health: a manual of bioenergetic exercises. Bioenergetics Press.

Lucas, J. (2011, June 10). Understanding your fascia (June 10, 2011). Retrieved from http://runningtimes.com/Article.aspx?ArticleID=23045&PageNum=2

Male pelvic floor: advanced massage and bodywork. http://www.malepelvicfloor.com/

Masich, S. Distinguishing the hip and waist. Retrieved February 26, 2013 from http://www.embracethemoon.com/perspectives/hip_waist.htm

MediLawTV. (2011, April 26). Pelvic anatomy sacro-iliac joint physical therapy animations [Video File}. Retrieved from http://www.youtube.com/watch?v=xxktB0kqIeY

Messelink, B., Benson, T., Berghmans, B. ... (2005). Standardization of terminology of pelvic floor muscle function and dysfunction: report from the pelvic floor clinical assessment group of the international continence society. *Neurourology and Urodynamics*

24:374-380. http://www.cofemer.fr/userfiles/Standardisation_ICS-05.pdf

Methodist Physicians Clinic. Pelvic floor dysfunction. Retrieved Feb Feb 26, 2013 from http://www.methodistsexualwellness.com/patient-information/glossary/pelvic-floor-dysfunction/

Miersch, L. (2011, September 27). Touching your toes means squat. Mobility is the new flexibility. Message posted to http://q.equinox.com/articles/2011/09/stretchingsecrets

Morin, J. (1998). Anal pleasure and health: a guide for men and women. San Fransisco, CA: Down There Press.

Myers, T. (2003).The deep six, part 1 (Originally published in Massage & Bodywork magazine, June/July 2003). Retrieved from http://www.massagetherapy.com/articles/index.php/article_id/412/The-Deep-Six-Part-1

Newton, F. & MacGregor, C. (1948). Spasm and fibrosis of the sphincter and due to reflex action. *New England Journal of Medicine, July; v.239, no.4. pgs:113-116.*

Nordin, M. Hirsch, V. (2012). Basic biomechanics of the musculoskeletal system. 4th edition. Baltimore, MD: Lippincott Williams, & Wilkins

NOVA. (2010). Physics of stone arches. Retrieved Feb 26, 2013 from http://www.teachersdomain.org/asset/nv37_int_arches/

Palmer, D. (2007). Qigong fever: body, science and utopia in china. 1st edition. New York, N.Y: Columbia University Press.

Pamela Morrison Physical Therapy. Anismus. Retrieved February 26, 2013 from http://www.pamelamorrisonpt.com/linkpage1.php?link=_665#pelvicpain

Pemberton, J., Swash, M., Henry, M. (eds.). (2002). *The pelvic floor: its function and disorders.* London; New York : W.B. Saunders.

Pool-Goudzwaard, A. & Hoek Van Dijke, G. & Van Gurp, M. & Mulder, P. & Snijders, C. & Stoeckart, R. (2004). Contribution of pelvic floor muscles to stiffness of the pelvic ring. *Clinical Biomechanics. Volume: 19, Issue: 6,* pgs: 564-571.

Ralston, P. (1999). Cheng hsin: the principles of effortless power. North Atlantic Books; 2nd edition.

References

Ralston, P. (2006). Zen body-being: an enlightened approach to physical skill, grace, and power. Berkeley, CA: Frog Ltd.

Ranaudo, K. (2008. February 12). The muscles of the pelvic floor. Message posted to http://www.pilatesdigest.com/the-muscles-of-the-pelvic-floor/

Raizada, V. & Mittal, R.(2008). Pelvic floor anatomy and applied physiology. *Gastroenterol Clin North Am. 2008 September; 37(3)*: 493–vii. http://www.ncbi.nlm.nih.gov/pmc/articles/PMC2617789/

Royer, D. (1920). Case of temporary incarceration of transverse colon within bilateral hernial sacs. *Indiana State Medical Association Journal, Fort Wayne July 15, 1920, 13, No. 7 page 227.* In *Journal of the American Medical Association,* Volume 75, Issues 1-13, (1920). Pg. 565.

Rummer, E. (2012, August 29) Why kegels are bad for your tight pelvic floor. Message posted to http://www.pelvicpainrehab.com/blog/2012/08/why-kegels-are-bad-for-your-pelvic-floor/

Saadah, O., Oliver, M., Bines, J., Stokes, K., Cameron, D. (2003). Case report: anorectal strictures and genital crohn disease: an unusual clinical association. *Journal of Pediatric Gastroenterology and Nutrition 36:403–406.*

Sapsford, R. & DipPhty & Hodges, P. (August 2001). Contraction of the pelvic floor muscles during abdominal maneuvers. *Archives of Physical Medicine and Rehabilitation. Vol 82. Issue 8.* pgs. 1081-1088.

Sapsford, R. & Hodges, P. (2001). Co-activation of the abdominal and pelvic floor muscles during voluntary exercises. *Neurourology and Urodynamics 20:31–42.*

Scarborough, W. (1875, 2013). A collection of chinese proverbs. CreateSpace Independent Publishing Platform.

Schafer, R.C., & Faye, L.J. (1989). Motion palpation and chiropractic technic (Principles of Dynamic Chiropractic), First edition. Chapter 6: The Pelvis. Retrieved from http://www.chiro.org/ACAPress/The_Pelvis.html

Schultz,R. (1999). Out in the open: the complete male pelvis. Berkeley, CA: North Atlantic Books.

Scribd.com (2009, July 23). Biomechanics of the hip. Retrieved February 26, 2013 from www.scribd.com/doc/17603002/Bio-Mechanics-Mechanics-of-the-Hip

Shengli, L. (2006). Combat techniques of taiji, xingyi, and bagua: principles and practices of internal martial arts. Berkeley, CA: Blue Snake Books.

SI BONE. (2011, November 29). SI joint anatomy, biomechanics & prevalence [Video File]. Retrieved from http://www.youtube.com/watch?v=D6NTMgWCSaU

SI Bone. (2011, November 29). SI joint anatomy, biomechanics & prevalence [Video File]. Retrieved from http://www.youtube.com/watch?v=D6NTMgWCSaU

Sigman, M. (1993). Training tip #1: The components of relaxing. *Internal Strength: A Practical Approach to Internal Strength and Qi*. Message posted at http://ismag.iay.org.uk/issue-1/training-tip.htm

Sigman, M. (1994). Training tip #6: using the waist. *Internal strength: a practical approach to internal strength and qi*. Retrieved from http://ismag.iay.org.uk/issue-6/training-tip.htm

Sim, D. & Gaffney, D. (2001). Chen style taijiquan: the source of taiji boxing. Berkeley, CA: Blue Snake Books.

Smith, E. (2000). The body in psychotherapy. Jefferson, NC: Mcfarland & Co Inc.

Society News. (1909). *Texas State Journal of Medicine, Vol 5, No 7, November 1909. p 291.*

Summers, K. What happens when we stretch? Retrieved February 26, 2013 from http://theyogadr.com/stretch/#more-1634

Taracks, R. (2009, June 21). Basic tips for zhan zhuang and the pelvis. Retrieved from http://wujifaliangong.blogspot.com/2009/06/basic-tips-for-zhan-zhang-and-pelvis.html

TCM_xiaozhong, (2008, December 12). The eight skills of taiji. Message posted to http://tcmdiscovery.com/Taiji/info/20081212_11497.html

Todd, M. (1937). The thinking body: a study of the balancing forces of dynamic man. Highstown, NJ: Princeton Book Co.

References

TheAnatomyZone. (2013, February 2). Pelvic floor part 1 - the pelvic diaphragm - 3D anatomy tutorial [Video File]. Retrieved from http://www.youtube.com/watch?v=P3BBAMWm2Eo

TheAnatomyZone. (2012, January 20). Muscles of the Thigh and Gluteal Region - Part 1 – Anatomy Tutorial. Retrieved from http://www.youtube.com/watch?v=kXg3akhbrrg

TheAnatomyZone. (2012, January 20). Muscles of the Thigh and Gluteal Region - Part 2 - Anatomy Tutorial. Retrieved from http://www.youtube.com/watch?v=ecfssWS1aVg

Thibodeaux, W. What is a rectal dilator? Retrieved February 26, 2013 from http://www.wisegeek.com/what-is-a-rectal-dilator.htm

Toilet-Related-Ailments.com. Pudendal nerve - mission control center for pelvic organs. Retrieved February 26, 2013 from http://www.toilet-related-ailments.com/pudendal-nerve.html

Ulrich, C. (August/Winter 2005). Freedom for feelings: bodywork and emotional release. *Massagetherapy.com*. http://www.massagetherapy.com/articles/index.php/article_id/940/Freedom-for-Feelings

Vaz, G., Roussouly, P., Berthonnaud, E., Dimnet, J. (2002). Sagittal morphology and equilibrium of pelvis and spine. *European Spine Journal*, Volume 11, Issue 1, pp 80-87.

Venable, C. (1915). Stricture of the Rectum. *Texas State Journal of Medicine. Vol 11, No 8, December 1915 pgs.441-442.*

Wang, S. (1978). Bagua linked palms. English version translated by Kent Howard and Hsiao-Yan Chen, 2009. Berkeley, CA: Blue Snake Books.

Wang, S. (1981). Bagua swimming body palms. English version translated by Kent Howard and Hsiao-Yan Chen, 2011. Berkeley, CA: Blue Snake Books.

Wang, X. 王西安, (1998). Chen family taijiquan tuishou (太极拳推手技法陈式). English version translated by Zhang Yanping, 2009. English edition. Australia: INBI Matrix Pty Ltd.

Whorton, J. (2000). Chapter 6: the culture of the abdomen: physical therapies. In *Inner Hygiene: Constipation and the Pursuit of Health in Modern Society* (pp. 141-145). New York. Oxford University Press.

Wise, D. & Anderson, R. (2011). A headache in the pelvis: a new understanding and treatment for chronic pelvic pain syndromes. 6th edition. Occidental, CA: National Center for Pelvic Pain Research.

Wood, M. (July 12 2008). Six breathing practices. http://bewellqigong.blogspot.com/2008/07/six-breathing-practices.html

Wright, R. (March 7, 2011). Nei dan meditation training. http://www.energygatesqigong.info/exercises-meditation/nei-dan-meditation-training.html

Wu, G. and Bisio, T. (2007). The essentials of ba gua zhang. New York, NY: New York Internal Arts.

Xiang, G. (2011). Authentic xing yi quan by gong zhong xiang. English version translated by Franklin Fick. CreateSpace Independent Publishing Platform.

Xu, X. (2000). Qigong for treating common ailments: The essential guide to self-healing. Boston, MA: YMAA Publication Center.

Yang, J. (2005). Qigong massage: fundamental techniques for health and relaxation. Wolfeboro, NH. YMAA Publishing Center, Inc.

Yang, J. (1998). The essence of taiji qigong: the internal foundation of taijiquan. Boston, MA: YMAA Publishing Center.

Yang, J. (2006). Qigong meditation: small circulation. Boston, MA: YMAA Publishing Center.

Yang, J. (1997). The root of chinese qigong: secrets of health, longevity, & enlightenment. Roslindale, MA: YMAA Publishing Center.

Young's Rectal Dilator, ca1925. Historical Research Center Digital Collections. Retrieved from http://hrcdigitalcoll.uams.edu/cdm/singleitem/collection/uw/id/682/rec/1

Yudelove, E. (1997). 100 days to better health, good sex and long life: a guide to taoist yoga & chi kung. St. Paul, MN: Llewellyn Publications.

Zhang, J. (2008). Liu bin's zhuang gong bagua zhang: south district beijing's strongly rooted style. Berkeley, CA: Blue Snake Books

Zmachinsky, W. The anal peripheral prostate massage. Retrieved February 26, 2013 from http://www.prostate-massage-and-health.com/Anal-peripheral-prostate-massage.html

Printed in Poland
by Amazon Fulfillment
Poland Sp. z o.o., Wrocław